The NO-NONSENSE GUIDE to

GLOBALIZATION

'Publishers have created lists of short books that discuss the questions that your average [electoral] candidate will only ever touch if armed with a slogan and a soundbite. Together [such books] hint at a resurgence of the grand educational tradition... Closest to the hot headline issues are *The No-Nonsense Guides*. These target those topics that a large army of voters care about, but that politicos evade. Arguments, figures and documents combine to prove that good journalism is far too important to be left to (most) journalists.'

Boyd Tonkin,
The Independent,
London

About the author
Wayne Ellwood established the North American office of *New Internationalist* in 1977 and was a co-editor of the magazine until 2010. He lives in Toronto where he now works as a freelance editorial consultant and writer.

About the New Internationalist
The **New Internationalist** is an independent not-for-profit publishing co-operative. Our mission is to report on issues of global justice. We publish informative current affairs and popular reference titles, complemented by world food, photography and gift books as well as calendars, diaries, maps and posters – all with a global justice world view.

If you like this *No-Nonsense Guide* you'll also love the **New Internationalist** magazine. Each month it tackles a range of subjects, from Iraq to Population, Climate Justice to Islam in Power, exploring each issue in a concise way which is easy to understand. The main articles are packed with photos, charts and graphs, and each magazine also contains music, film and book reviews, country profiles, interviews and news.

To find out more about the **New Internationalist**, visit our website at
www.newint.org

The **NO-NONSENSE GUIDE** to

GLOBALIZATION

Wayne Ellwood

New Internationalist

The No-Nonsense Guide to Globalization
Published in the UK in 2010 by New Internationalist™ Publications Ltd
New Internationalist™ Publications Ltd
Oxford OX4 1BW, UK
www.newint.org
New Internationalist is a registered trade mark.

Original edition 2001; second edition 2006, with reprints in 2007 and 2009.

Cover image: Justin Guariglia/Corbis

Series editor: Chris Brazier
Design by New Internationalist Publications Ltd.

Printed by T J International Limited, Cornwall, UK
who hold environmental accreditation ISO 14001.

Mixed Sources
Product group from well-managed
forests and other controlled sources
www.fsc.org   Cert no. SGS-COC-2482
© 1996 Forest Stewardship Council

British Library Cataloguing-in-Publication Data.
A catalogue record for this book is available from the British Library.

Library of Congress Cataloguing-in-Publication Data.
A catalogue for this book is available from the Library of Congress.

ISBN: 978-1-906523-47-3

Foreword

THIS IS AN important work for anyone concerned about the future of planetary life. It is a clear and richly factual overview of the global corporate system – from its colonial past beginning with Cristóbal Colón's famous 1492 search for a sea route to the fabled riches of East Asia, to the current regime of 'globalization' in which a comprehensive plan to subordinate domestic economies everywhere to transnational banking and corporate rule is now into high gear.

Ceaseless repetition of slogans of 'inevitable change' and 'necessary restructuring' have everywhere accompanied this rapid prying-open of national economies and cultures for foreign exploitation 'free of trade and investment barriers'. But there is an astonishing gap between the dominant ideology of a 'self-regulating global free market' and the reality of tens of thousands of trade-lawyer constructed regulations imposed across the world by a fast-moving, secretive process instituting the private demands of transnational corporations as absolute rights to which elected legislatures everywhere are made subordinate.

The fact is that the very opposite of a 'free market' is at work. Since the fall of the Berlin Wall, corporate financial interests and their mass media vehicles have together stormed governments with an overwhelming agenda for world corporate rule. The rules are political, but unspoken. Either governments competitively enact this agenda, or deregulated capital and election funding will go elsewhere and resistant leaders will be ignored or pilloried in the corporate press.

The public is reassured that 'a rising tide of growth will lift all boats'. The demand is that 'global market competition be made free of the tax and regulatory burdens of government'. But the harsh reality is the very opposite of rising standards of living and new freedoms for the world's peoples. On almost every indicator of social and ecological life – from health protection, literacy development and future vocations for the young to maintenance of biodiversity and the planet's security of air, water, soil and climate – the restructuring of societies for corporate globalization has been increasingly life-destructive.

This book's wide-lensed and well-informed coverage of the system's global operations exposes the life-blind economics at work in a graphic explanation of what is really going on. If there is to be a turning of global governance towards true sustainability, we need to recognize that it has to be in a direction that makes civil and planetary life sovereign instead of instrumentalizing both for the money-to-more-money feeding cycle of transnational financial interests.

This policy itself, in turn, can only be achieved by people awakening in large numbers to the spectacularly failed program of corporate globalization. *The No-Nonsense Guide to Globalization* provides a lucid explanatory map of our current condition. For all who seek to think past corporate slogans to life-responsible government, this is a concise and valuable overview of the world system, what has gone wrong with it – and the way ahead.

Professor John McMurtry,
Department of Philosophy,
University of Guelph,
Ontario, Canada.

CONTENTS

Introduction

WHEN THE FIRST edition of this book was published more than a decade ago I described globalization as 'the most talked-about and perhaps the least understood concept of the new millennium'.

Much has happened in the intervening 10 years. The world has changed in quite stunning ways. Globalization was a relatively new word back then. Today, library shelves are groaning with countless texts on the subject. The fallout is everywhere – nowhere more evident than in the devastating collapse of the global economy that began in 2007/08 and whose repercussions continue to be felt today.

But before that came the tragic, criminal attacks of September 11, 2001 – a day that changed the course of world history and underlined, with murderous irony, the increasing contradictions of a globalized world. As national and regional economies become more intertwined, the idea of a global community with shared goals and values appears to be fading. In response to the September 11 attacks, the US and its allies launched a protracted 'war on terror' which flouted both domestic and international law. As a consequence, attempts to address the root causes of terrorism – poverty, political exclusion and growing inequality – have largely been shelved.

Since the autumn of 2008 the wars in Iraq, Afghanistan, Pakistan and the simmering conflict in Israel/Palestine have been fought against a backdrop of global economic collapse.

We are now living through the most serious economic crisis since the Great Depression of the 1930s.

The link to globalization, specifically to the world-wide deregulation of the finance and banking sectors, is visible to all. (The history of this shift to a 'global casino' built on lax government regulation of these industries is outlined in Chapter 5.) Facing catastrophe, governments stepped into the breach with hundreds of billions in taxpayer funds to bail out the banks and keep the credit system solvent. They also ploughed billions into classic Keynesian stimulus packages to fend off complete economic collapse. Even once-powerful icons of the industrial era like General Motors (GM) came cap-in-hand in search of government handouts. (GM received a total of $50 billion from Washington. The government got $2 billion in stock and 61 per cent of the company's privately held common shares in return for the rest of the money.) AIG, the largest insurance company in the US, swallowed more than $180 billion in public funds. In total the amounts the UK and the US earmarked to support their banks reached nearly 75 per cent of their combined GDP.

The cost in jobs, hunger, poverty and fear has been incalculable – what one US analyst describes as 'a slow-motion social catastrophe... that could stain our culture and weaken our nation for many, many years.'[1]

In a recent analysis of the impact of the global crisis the UN Development Programme notes:

- The International Labour Organization projects that over 50 million more people became unemployed in 2009. The ranks of the working poor – people working and living on less than $2 a day – jumped by over 200 million.
- The Mine Workers Union of Zambia estimates that 10,000 out of a total 23,000 miners will be laid off.
- 200,000 Indonesian nationals previously working in Malaysia returned home in 2008 as a result of the recession, with most of them women from the country's rural areas.
- In China, over 20 million domestic migrant workers were laid off in early 2009.
- In Ghana, the Ministry of Finance estimates that foreign remittances were down by over $50 million in January 2009 compared with one year before.[2]

Introduction

Despite the economic and human carnage, the bankers appear to have learned little. They have furiously opposed more stringent regulation at every step. And governments, for the most part, have been reluctant to introduce tough new regulations, or to enforce existing ones. America's first black President, the oratorically gifted Barack Obama, rode to victory in November 2008 on the promise of hope and sweeping change. So far rhetoric has outstripped action – despite promises to rein in 'proprietary trading' (making risky bets on investments for the bank's own profit). Wall Street appears to have cowed even the US President. Executives at US financial firms shamelessly scooped up more than $20 billion in bonuses in 2009, the same year the companies received trillions in government support.

The recent economic meltdown has left critics more determined than ever to reshape globalization into a force for improving the lives of the majority of the world's people.

Across Latin America the electorate has embraced democracy and rejected a free trade model which has sacked national economies, subverted local cultures and thrown millions into poverty and unemployment. In Greece, in early 2010, protesters reacted with outrage and violence to government moves to slash public spending in the face of a debt crisis brought on by the global economic crisis. The press began referring to the Greek uprising as 'the first credit-crunch riot'.[3]

At the international level there has been encouraging progress in building institutions that reinforce global citizenship and bolster international law – however imperfect. The UN Ban on Landmines, the International Tribunals on Former Yugoslavia and Rwanda and the International Criminal Court are three such initiatives. Meanwhile, at Copenhagen in December 2009, the world fumbled an opportunity to replace the Kyoto Protocol on Climate Change with a serious program to combat global warming.

The reality of globalization may have entered public consciousness during the last decade but the concept is as old as capitalism itself – a continuing saga of shifting markets and melding cultures. The world has been shrinking for centuries. Peppers, maize and potatoes, once found only in Latin America, are now common foods in India, Africa and Europe. Spices originally from Indonesia thrive in the Caribbean. The descendants of black Africans, first brought as slaves to work the land of the 'new world', have become Americans, Jamaicans, Canadians, Brazilians and Guyanese.

But the 'old story' of globalization has today developed a new twist sparked by technological change. The micro-electronics revolution of the past 25 years has irrevocably altered the essence of human communication. Digital technology has forged a world of instant communications, creating what some have called the 'third wave' of economic growth.

The computer revolution that has boosted the new global economy has also been used in other, sometimes contradictory, ways. Images of conflict and violence can spread with lightning speed as opponents of globalization use email and mobile phones to share information, strategize across international borders and organize demonstrations. The horrific torture of prisoners by US troops in Abu Ghraib prison; the stark videos of sobbing, frightened hostages in Iraq; the inflammatory Danish cartoons that sparked worldwide protests; the rise of the World Social Forum; the global demonstrations against climate change; the proliferation of grassroots citizens' movements. All are in some way the fruits of globalization.

Just as technology can stoke the fires of dissent and amplify events which once might have remained unknown, so the speed of global travel has turned the whole world into ground zero for lethal new diseases.

Introduction

The deadly SARS epidemic in 2003 reached 31 countries in less than a month. In 2009, the H1N1 influenza virus caromed around the globe after its initial discovery in Mexico, spreading panic and raising fears of a global pandemic. The World Health Organization predicts that the avian flu virus, if it crosses to humans, could kill up to seven million people worldwide. The globalization of trade and the industrialization of animal husbandry are intimately linked to the spread of these new diseases.

This global exchange of people, products, plants, animals, technologies and ideas will continue for the foreseeable future – even if our dependence on fossil fuels decreases. The process of change is unstoppable.

Despite the dangers, this new, more intimate world holds much promise. If we jointly recognize the common thread of humanity that ties us together, how can globalization not be a positive force for change?

The Western tradition is steeped in optimism and the notion of progress. The basic credo is simple: growth is the measure of human development and the vision of a globally unified market is the ultimate goal. The expansion of international trade will lead to a more equal, more peaceful, less parochial world. Eventually, so the argument goes, global integration and cross-cultural understanding will create a borderless world where political parochialisms are put aside in a new pact of shared universal humanity.

This is a compelling vision – we live in a world of enormous wealth and great opportunity. Despite the recent recession, there are now more people living longer, healthier, more productive lives than at any time in human history. And much of that is due to the extraordinary capacity of industrial capitalism to produce the goods.

But this success has been compromised by a corporate-led plan for economic integration which threatens cultural uniqueness, economic independence and political sovereignty. Instead of helping to build a better world for all, the fundamentalist free-market model is eroding both democracy and equity. The social goals, the cohesive values that make us work as communities, are being ignored in the headlong rush to break down the barriers to trade.

The global economy teeters on the brink, gaps between rich and poor are widening, decision-making power is concentrated in fewer and fewer hands, local cultures are homogenized, biological diversity is destroyed, regional tensions are increasing and the environment is nearing the point of collapse. That is the face of globalization today, an opportunity for human progress whose potential has been denied.

This *No-Nonsense Guide* attempts to sketch an admittedly incomplete picture of that global economic system – its history, its structure, its failings – and the forces in whose interest it works.

By understanding how we got here and what is at stake, we can perhaps find a route out of the current economic crisis and in the process redefine globalization. The solutions are by no means definite. But there is a lively debate. The events of the past few years only bolster the conclusion that radical change is long overdue.

Wayne Ellwood
Toronto, March 2010

1 'How a new jobless era will transform America', Don Peck, *The Atlantic*, March 2010. **2** UN Development Programme, 'The economic crisis around the world', www.undp.org/economic_crisis/index.shtml **3** Ed Vulliamy and Helena Smith, 'Children of the revolution', *The Observer*, 22 Feb 2010.

1 Globalization then and now

Globalization is a new word which describes an old process: the integration of the global economy that began in earnest with the launch of the European colonial era five centuries ago. But the process has accelerated over the past 30 years with the explosion of computer technology, the dismantling of barriers to the movement of goods and capital, and the expanding political and economic power of transnational corporations.

MORE THAN FIVE centuries ago, in a world without electricity, cellphones, refrigeration, DVDs, the internet, automobiles, airplanes or nuclear weapons, one man had a foolish dream. Or so it seemed at the time. Cristóbal Colón, an ambitious young Genoese sailor and adventurer, was obsessed with Asia – a region about which he knew nothing, apart from unsubstantiated rumors of its colossal wealth. Such was the strength of his obsession (some say his greed) that he was able to convince the King and Queen of Spain to finance a voyage into the unknown across a dark, seemingly limitless expanse of water then known as the Ocean Sea. His goal: to find the Grand Khan of China and the gold that was reportedly there in profusion.

Centuries later, Colón would become familiar to millions of schoolchildren across the West as Christopher Columbus, the famous 'discoverer' of the Americas. In fact, the 'discovery' was more of an accident. The intrepid Columbus never did reach Asia, not even close. Instead, after five weeks at sea, he found himself sailing under a tropical sun into the turquoise waters of the Caribbean, making his landfall somewhere in the Bahamas, which he promptly named San Salvador (the Savior). The place clearly delighted Columbus' weary crew. They loaded up with fresh water and unusual foodstuffs. And they were befriended by the island's indigenous population, the Taino.

'They are the best people in the world and above all the gentlest,' Columbus wrote in his journal. 'They very willingly showed my people where the water was, and they themselves carried the full barrels to the boat, and took great delight in pleasing us. They became so much our friends that it was a marvel.'[1]

Twenty years and several voyages later, most of the Taino were dead and the other indigenous peoples of the Caribbean were either enslaved or under attack. Globalization, even then, had moved quickly from an innocent process of cross-cultural exchange to a nasty scramble for wealth and power. As local populations died off from European diseases or were literally worked to death by their captors, thousands of European colonizers followed. Their desperate quest was for gold and silver. But the conversion of heathen souls to the Christian faith gave an added fillip to their plunder. Eventually European settlers colonized most of the new lands to the north and south of the Caribbean.

Columbus' adventure in the Americas was notable for many things, not least his focus on extracting as much wealth as possible from the land and the people. But, more importantly, his voyages opened the door to 450 years of European colonialism. And it was this centuries-long imperial era that laid the groundwork for today's global economy.

Old globalization

Although globalization has become a commonplace term in recent years, many people would be hard pressed to define what it actually means. The lens of history provides a useful beginning. Globalization is an age-old process and one firmly rooted in the experience of colonialism. One of Britain's most famous imperial figures, Cecil Rhodes, put the case for colonialism succinctly in the 1890s. 'We must find new lands,' he said, 'from which we can easily obtain raw materials and at the same time exploit the cheap slave labor that is available from the natives of the colonies. The colonies [will] also provide a dumping ground for the surplus goods produced in our factories.'[2]

During the colonial era, European nations spread their rule across the globe. The British, French, Dutch, Spanish, Portuguese, Belgians, Germans, and later the Americans, took possession of most of what was later called the Third World. And, of course, they also expanded into Australia, New Zealand/Aotearoa and North America. In some places (the Americas, Australia, New Zealand and southern Africa) they did so with the intent of establishing new lands for European settlement. Elsewhere (Africa and Asia) their interest was more in the spirit of Rhodes' vision: markets and plunder. From 1600 to 1800 incalculable riches were siphoned out of Latin America as it became the chief source of finance for Europe's industrial revolution.

Global trade expanded rapidly during the colonial period as European powers sucked in raw materials from their new dominions: furs, timber and fish from Canada; slaves and gold from Africa; sugar, rum and fruits from the Caribbean; coffee, sugar, meat, gold and silver from Latin America; opium, tea and spices from Asia. Ships crisscrossed the oceans. Heading towards the colonies, their holds were filled with settlers and manufactured goods; returning home, the stout galleons and streamlined clippers bulged with coffee, copra and cocoa. By the 1860s and the 1870s, world trade was booming. It was a 'golden era' of international commerce – though the European powers pretty much stacked things in their favor. Wealth from their overseas colonies flooded into France, England, Holland and Spain but some of it also flowed back into the colonies as investment – into railways, roads,

Tyranny and poverty

Colonialism in the Americas separated Indians from their land, destroyed traditional economies and left native people among the poorest of the poor.

- The Spanish ran the Bolivian silver mines with a slave labor system known as the *mita*; nearly eight million Indians had died in the Potosí mines by 1650.
- Suicide and alcoholism are common responses to social dislocation. Suicide rates on Canadian Indian reserves are 10 to 20 times higher than the national average.
- In Guatemala life expectancy for non-natives is 61 years; for Indians it is 45. The infant mortality rate for Indian children is twice that of non-Indians (160 deaths per thousand versus 80). ■

Indian Population of the Americas: 1492 and 1992

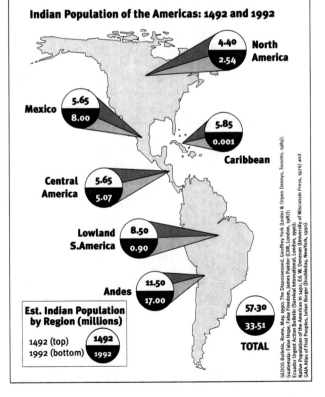

North America
4.40
2.54

Mexico
5.65
8.00

Caribbean
5.85
0.001

Central America
5.65
5.07

Lowland S. America
8.50
0.90

Andes
11.50
17.00

Est. Indian Population by Region (millions)

1492 (top)
1992 (bottom)

1492
1992

TOTAL
57.30
33.51

SEDOS Bulletin, Rome, May, 1990; The Dispossessed, Geoffrey York (Lester & Orpen Dennys, Toronto, 1989); Guatemala: False Hope, False Freedom, James Painter (CIIR, London, 1987); Ecuador Urgent Action Bulletin (Survival International, London, 1990); Native Population of the Americas in 1492, Ed. W. Denevan (University of Wisconsin Press, 1976) and GAIA Atlas of First Peoples, Julian Burger (Doubleday, NewYork, 1990).

ports, dams and cities. Such was the range of global commerce in the 19th century that capital transfers from North to South were actually greater in real terms at the end of the 1890s than at the end of the 1990s. By 1913, exports (one of the hallmarks of increasing economic integration) accounted for a larger share of global production than they did in 1999.

When people talk about globalization today, they're still talking mostly about economics, about an expanding international trade in goods and services based on the concept of 'comparative advantage'. This theory was first developed in 1817 by the British economist David Ricardo in his *Principles of Political Economy and Taxation*. Ricardo wrote that nations should specialize in producing goods in which they have a natural advantage and thereby find their market niche. He believed this would benefit both buyer and seller but only if certain conditions were maintained, namely that:

1) Trade between partners must be balanced so that one country doesn't become indebted and dependent on another.
2) Investment capital must be anchored locally and not allowed to flow from a high-wage country to a low-wage country.

Unfortunately, in today's high-tech world of instant communications, neither of these key conditions exists. The result: Ricardo's vision of local self-reliance mixed with balanced exports and imports is nowhere to be seen. Instead, export-led trade dominates the global economic agenda. Increasingly, the only route to greater prosperity is based on expanding exports to the rest of the world.

The rationale is that all countries and all peoples eventually benefit from the results of increased trade. In the teeth of the 2008-2009 economic crisis, world trade slumped for the first time in living memory. According to the World Trade Organization, trade levels in Europe fell by nearly 16 per cent in the fourth quarter of 2008 while global trade fell by more than 30 per cent in the first quarter of 2009. But world trade had zoomed ahead in the previous decade. It grew at an average 6.6 per cent during the 1990s and at more than 6 per cent a year in the post-millennium period. Global trade was actually growing faster than total world output. This expansion increased global income by more than $500 billion. Unfortunately, most of this wealth ended up in the hands of the industrialized nations. They account for the lion's share of world trade and they mostly trade with each other. Indeed, the rich world accounts for almost two-thirds of global merchandise exports, a figure which has remained more or less steady since 1960. The share of Latin America, Central/Eastern Europe and Africa in total world exports was lower in 2002 than in 1960.[3]

Nonetheless, the world has changed in the last century in ways that have completely altered the character of the global economy and its impact on people and the natural world. Today's globalization is vastly different from both the colonial era and the immediate post-World War Two period. Even arch-capitalists like currency speculator George Soros have voiced doubts about the negative values that underlie the direction of the modern global economy.

'Insofar as there is a dominant belief in our society today,' he writes, 'it is a belief in the magic of the marketplace. The doctrine of laissez-faire capitalism holds that the common good is best served by the uninhibited pursuit of self-interest... Unsure of what they stand for, people increasingly rely on money as the criterion of value... The cult of success has replaced a belief in principles. Society has lost its anchor.'

Market magic
The 'magic of the marketplace' is not a new concept. It's been around in one form or another since the father

Globalization then and now

of modern economics, Adam Smith, first published his pioneering work *The Wealth of Nations* in 1776. Coincidentally, in the same year Britain's 13 restless American colonies declared independence from the motherland. But Smith's concept of the market was a far cry from the one championed by today's globalization boosters. Smith was adamant that markets worked most efficiently when there was equality between buyer and seller, and when neither was large enough to influence the market price. This, he said, would ensure that all parties received a fair return and that society as a whole would benefit through the best use of its natural and human resources. Smith also believed that capital was best invested locally so that owners could see what was happening with their

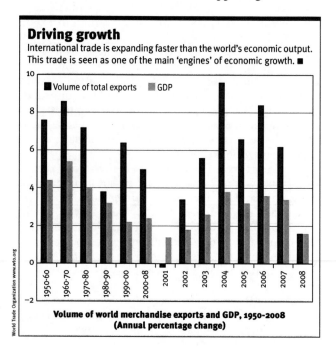

Driving growth

International trade is expanding faster than the world's economic output. This trade is seen as one of the main 'engines' of economic growth. ■

Volume of world merchandise exports and GDP, 1950-2008 (Annual percentage change)

World Trade Organization www.wto.org

investment and could have hands-on management of its use. Author and activist David Korten sums up Smith's thinking as follows:

'His vision of an efficient market was one composed of small owner-managed enterprises located in the communities where the owners resided. Such owners would share in the community's values and have a personal stake in its future. It is a market that has little in common with a globalized economy, dominated by massive corporations without local or national allegiance, managed by professionals who are removed from real owners by layers of investment institutions and holding companies.'[4]

As Korten hints, today's world is vastly different from the one that Adam Smith inhabited. Take the revolution in communications technology which began around 1980. In just 30 years, computers, fiber-optics, satellites and microprocessors have radically altered the production, sales and distribution of goods and services, as well as patterns of global investment. Coupled with improvements in air freight and ocean transport, companies can now move their plants and factories to wherever costs are lowest. Being close to the target market is no longer crucial. Improved technology and relatively inexpensive oil (for the moment anyway) has led to a massive increase in goods being transported by air and sea. World air traffic cargo tripled from 1985 to 1997 and, before the recent downturn, was predicted to triple again by 2015. The Council of the International Civil Aviation Organization (ICAO) notes that about two billion passengers and 44 million tons of freight were carried by the world's airlines in 2005, a 44 and 74 per cent increase respectively over 10 years. (By contrast passenger traffic declined by 3.1 per cent in 2009, the largest slide on record, reflecting the one per cent drop in the world gross domestic product for that year. Cargo traffic plummeted by 15 per cent following the drop in world trade.) The global shipping business, which now consumes more than 140 million tons of fuel oil a year, is expected to rebound dramatically once the global economy gets back on track. And costs are falling.

According to the Washington-based World Shipping Council, approximately 1,500 shipping companies make 26,000 US port calls a year while more than 50,000 container loads of imports and exports from 175 countries are handled each day. From 1990 to 2005, freight costs on the three major US trade shipping routes fell by between 23 and 46 per cent. In 2000, US exporters spent about $3 billion less than they did in 1985 to ship their goods to market – extraordinary, considering that there was 65 per cent inflation over that same period. Ocean freight unit costs have fallen by 70 per cent since the 1980s while air freight costs have fallen by three to four per cent a year on average over the last two decades.

These transport rates in reality are 'cheap' only in a financial sense. They may reflect 'internal' costs – packaging, marketing, labor, debt and profit. But they don't reflect the 'external' impact on the environment of this massive use of irreplaceable fossil fuels. Moving more

Human Development Report 1999, UN Development Programme / Oxford University Press; Financial Frenzy, Liberalization, Speculation and Regulation, War on Want, London 1999.

Pinball capital

Short-term speculative capital whizzes around the world leaving ravaged economies and human devastation in its wake. East Asia (Indonesia, South Korea, Thailand, Malaysia, the Philippines) suffered a destructive net reversal of private capital flows from 1996 to 1997 of $12 billion.

Percentage change in GDP before and after the Asian financial crisis

	Thailand	Indonesia	Malaysia	S.Korea
Average 1980-90	7.6	6.1	5.2	9.4
Average 1990-96	8.3	7.7	8.7	7.3
Average 1997	-7	-16	-6	-6

goods around the planet increases pollution, contributes to ground-level ozone (smog) and boosts greenhouse gas emissions, a major source of global warming and climate change. These environmental costs are basically ignored in the profit-and-loss equation of business. This is one of the main reasons why environmentalists object to the globalization of trade. Companies make the profits but society has to foot the bill.

The other key factor which shaped globalization has to do with structural changes to the world economy since the early 1970s. It was then that the system of rules set up at the end of World War Two to manage global trade collapsed. The fixed currency-exchange regime agreed at Bretton Woods, New Hampshire, in 1944 gave the world 35 years of relatively steady economic growth.

Enter free-market fundamentalism
Around 1980, things began to shift with the emergence of fundamentalist free-market governments in Britain and the US, and the disintegration of the state-run command economy in the former Soviet Union. The formula for economic progress adopted

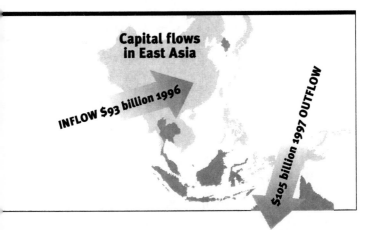

Capital flows in East Asia

INFLOW $93 billion 1996

$105 billion 1997 OUTFLOW

by the administrations of Margaret Thatcher in the UK and Ronald Reagan in the US called for a drastic reduction in the regulatory role of the state. According to their intellectual influences, Austrian economist Friedrich Hayek and University of Chicago academic Milton Friedman, meddlesome big government was the problem. Instead, government was to take its direction from the market. Companies must be free to move their operations anywhere in the world to minimize costs and maximize returns to investors. Free trade, unfettered investment, deregulation, balanced budgets, low inflation and privatization of publicly owned enterprises were trumpeted as the six-step plan to national prosperity.

The deregulation of world financial markets went hand-in-hand with an emphasis on free trade. Banks, insurance companies and investment dealers, whose operations had hitherto been mostly confined within national borders, were suddenly unleashed. Within a few years, the big players from Europe, Japan and North America had expanded into each other's markets as well as into the newly opened and fragile financial services markets in the Global South. Aided by sophisticated computer systems (which made it easy to transfer huge amounts of money at the click of a mouse) and governments desperate for investment, the big banks and investment houses were quick to invest surplus cash anywhere they could turn a profit. In this new relaxed atmosphere, finance capital became a profoundly destabilizing influence on the global economy.

Instead of long-term investment in the production of real goods and services, speculators in the global casino make money from money – with little concern for the impact of their investments on local communities or national economies. Governments everywhere now fear the destabilizing impact of this 'hot money'. The collapse of 2008-09 – the most devastating since the Great Depression of the 1930s – is just the

Third World

If there's a Third World, then there must be a First and Second World too. When the term was first coined in 1952 by the French demographer, Alfred Sauvy, there was a clear distinction, though the differences have become blurred over the past decade. Derived from the French phrase, *tiers monde*, the term was first used to suggest parallels between the *tiers monde* (the world of the poor countries) and the *tiers état* (the third estate or common people of the French revolutionary era). The First World was the North American/European 'Western bloc' while the Soviet-led 'Eastern bloc' was the Second World. These two groups had most of the economic and military power and faced off in a tense ideological confrontation commonly called the 'Cold War'. Third World countries in Africa, Latin America, Asia and the Pacific had just broken free of colonial rule and were attempting to make their own way rather than become entangled in the tug-of-war between East and West. Since the break-up of the Soviet Union in the early 1990s the term Third World has less meaning and its use is diminishing. Now many refer to the 'developing nations', the Majority World or just the South. ∎

latest in a long chain of financial disasters. Recent United Nations (UN) studies show a direct correlation between the frequency of financial crises around the world and the huge increase in international capital flows between 1990 and 2010.

The collapse of the East Asian currencies, which began in July 1997, was a catastrophic example of the damage caused by nervous short-term investors. Until then the 'Tiger Economies' of Thailand, Taiwan, Singapore, Malaysia and South Korea had been the success stories of globalization. Advocates of open markets pointed to these countries as proof that classic capitalism would bring wealth and prosperity to millions in the developing world – though they conveniently ignored the fact that in all these countries the State took a strong and active role in shaping the economy. According to dissident ex-World Bank Chief Economist, Joseph Stiglitz: 'The combination of high savings rates, government investment in education and state-directed industrial policy all served to make the region an economic powerhouse. Growth rates were phenomenal for decades and the standard of living rose enormously for tens of millions of people.'[5]

Foreign investment was tightly controlled by national governments until the early 1990s, severely in South Korea and Taiwan, less so in Thailand and Malaysia. Then, as a result of continued pressure from the International Monetary Fund (IMF) and others, the 'tigers' began to open up their capital accounts and private-sector businesses began to borrow heavily.

Spectacular growth rates floated on a sea of foreign investment as offshore investors poured dollars into the region, eager to harvest double-digit returns. In 1996, capital was flowing into East Asia at almost $100 billion a year. But mostly the cash went into risky real-estate ventures or onto the local stock market where it inflated share prices far beyond the value of their underlying assets.

In Thailand, where the Asian 'miracle' first began to sour, over-investment in real estate left the market glutted with $20 billion worth of new unsold properties. The house of cards collapsed when foreign investors began to realize that Thai financial institutions to which they had lent billions could not meet loan repayments. Spooked by the specter of falling profits and a stagnant real-estate market, investors called in their loans and cashed in their investments – first slowly, then in a panic-stricken rush.

More than $105 billion left the entire region in the next 12 months, equivalent to 11 per cent of the domestic output of the most seriously affected countries – Indonesia, the Philippines, South Korea, Thailand and Malaysia.[6] Having abandoned any kind of capital controls, Asian governments were powerless to stop the massive hemorrhage of funds. Ironically, the IMF's 1997 *Annual Report*, written just before the crisis, had singled out Thailand's 'remarkable economic performance' and 'consistent record of sound macroeconomic policies'.

The IMF was to be proven wrong – disastrously so. Across the region, economic output plummeted while unemployment soared, leaping by a factor of 10 in Indonesia alone. The human costs of the East Asian economic crisis were immediate and devastating. As bankruptcies soared, firms shut their doors and millions of workers were laid off. More than 400 Malaysian companies declared bankruptcy between July 1997 and March 1998 while in Indonesia – the poorest country affected by the crisis – 20 per cent of the population, nearly 40 million people, were pushed into poverty. The impact of the economic slowdown had the devastating effect of reducing both family income and government expenditures on social and health services for years afterwards. In Thailand, more than 100,000 children were yanked from school when parents could no longer afford tuition fees. The crash also had a knock-on effect outside Asia. Shockwaves rippled through Latin America, nearly tipping Brazil into recession. The Russian economy suffered even worse damage: growth rates slipped into reverse and the Russian ruble became nearly worthless as a medium of international exchange.

The East Asian crisis was a serious blow to the 'promise' of globalization – and a stiff challenge to the orthodox economic prescriptions of the IMF. Indeed, in retrospect, the Asian meltdown of 1997-98 can be seen as a warm-up for the debacle of 2007-09. Across the region, the Fund was reviled as the source of economic disaster. The citizens of East Asia saw their interests ignored in favor of Western banks and investors. In the end, writes Stiglitz: 'It was the IMF policies which undermined the market as well as the long-run stability of the economy and society.' It was the first time that the 'global managers' and finance kingpins showed that the system wasn't all it was made out to be. The world economy was more fragile, and thus more explosive, than anybody had imagined. As the region slowly recovered, citizens around the world began to scratch their heads and wonder about the pros and cons of globalization, especially the wisdom of unregulated investment. The mass public protests against the World Trade Organization, the IMF/ World Bank and the G8 were still to come – in Seattle, Prague, Genoa, Quebec City, Doha and elsewhere. But the East Asian crisis planted worrying seeds of doubt about the merits of corporate globalization.

1 Kirkpatrick Sale, *The Conquest of Paradise: Christopher Columbus and the Columban Legacy*, Knopf, New York, 1990. **2** *The Ecologist*, Vol 29, No 3, May/June 1999. **3** *Development and Globalization: Facts and Figures 2004*, UNCTAD. **4** David Korten, *When Corporations Rule the World*, Kumarian/ Berrett-Koehler, West Hartford/San Francisco, 1995. **5** Joseph Stiglitz, *Globalization and its Discontents*, WW Norton, New York/London, 2003. **6** *Human Development Report 1999*, United Nations Development Programme, New York/Oxford, 1999.

2 The Bretton Woods Trio

The Great Depression of the 1930s leads to the birth of Keynesianism and the interventionist state. As World War Two ends, the victors put together a new set of rules for the global economy. This post-War financial architecture includes the World Bank, the International Monetary Fund (IMF) and the General Agreement on Tariffs and Trade (GATT). But, as Third World nations emerge from centuries of colonialism, these institutions are seen increasingly as pillars of the status quo.

AS WORLD WAR TWO was drawing to a close, the world's leading politicians and government officials, mostly from the victorious 'Allied' nations (mainly Britain, the United States, the Soviet Union, Canada, France, Australia and New Zealand) began to think about the need to establish a system of rules to run the post-War global economy.

Before the widespread outbreak of the 1939 War, trading nations everywhere had been racked by a crippling economic depression. When the US stock market crashed in October 1929 the shockwaves were felt around the world. Nations turned inward in an attempt to pull themselves out of a steep economic skid. But, without a system of global rules, there was no coherence or larger logic to the 'beggar-thy-neighbor' polices adopted worldwide. High tariff barriers were thrown up between countries, with the result that world trade nosedived, economic growth spluttered and mass unemployment and poverty followed. From 1929 to 1932, global trade fell by an astounding 62 per cent while global industrial production slumped by 36 per cent. As a result, the 1930s became a decade of radical politics and rancorous social ferment in the West as criticism of laissez-faire capitalism and an unchecked market economy grew.

The Bretton Woods trio

Scholars like Hungarian exile Karl Polanyi helped reinforce a growing suspicion of a market-based economic model which put money and investors at the center of its concerns rather than social values and human well-being. 'To allow the market mechanism to be the sole director of the fate of human beings and their natural environment... would result in the demolition of society,' Polanyi wrote in his masterwork, *The Great Transformation*.

Polanyi was not alone in his distrust of the market economy. Other thinkers, such as the influential British economist John Maynard Keynes, were also grappling with a way of controlling global markets, making them work for people and not the other way around. Keynes both admired and feared the power of the market system. With the example of the Great Depression of the 1930s fresh in his mind, he predicted that, without firm boundaries and controls, capitalism would be immobilized by its own greed, and would eventually self-destruct. As it happened, only World War Two turned things around. The War set the factories humming again as millions of troops were deployed by all sides in the conflict. Arms manufacturers, aircraft factories and other military suppliers ran 24-hour shifts, primed by government spending. Then, as the War wound down, government policy makers began to think about how to ensure a smooth transformation to a peacetime economy.

It was Keynes' radical notion of an 'interventionist' state to which governments turned in an effort to rebuild their economies. Until the worldwide slump of the 1930s, the accepted economic wisdom had been that a degree of unemployment was a 'normal condition' of the free market. The economy might go up or down according to the business cycle but in the long run growth (and increased global trade) would create new jobs and sop up the unemployed.

Keynes was skeptical of this *laissez-faire* (let it be)

orthodoxy, suggesting that the economy was a human-made artifact and that people acting together through their government could have some control over its direction. Why not act now, he suggested, since 'in the long run we're all dead'. With no other obvious solutions in the wings, his approach offered a way out for governments who found themselves helplessly mired in economic stagnation.

In *The General Theory of Employment, Interest and Money*, published in 1936, Keynes argued that the free market, left on its own, actually creates unemployment. Profitability, he said, depends on suppressing wages and cutting costs by replacing labor with technology. In other words, profits and a certain amount of unemployment go hand in hand – so far so good, at least for those making the profits. But Keynes went on to show that lowering wages and laying off workers would inevitably result in fewer people who could afford to buy the goods that factories were producing. As demand fell, so would sales; factory owners would be forced to lay off even more workers. This, reasoned Keynes, was the start of a downward spiral with terrible human consequences.

To 'prime the economic pump', Keynes suggested governments intervene actively in the economy. He reasoned that business owners and rich investors are unlikely to open their wallets if the prospects for profit look dim. When the economy is in a tailspin, Keynes argued that governments should step in – by spending on public goods (education, healthcare, job training) and on 'infrastructure' (roads, sewers, dams, public transport, electricity); and by giving direct financial support to the unemployed.

Even if governments had to go into debt to kick-start growth, Keynes advised politicians not to worry. The price was worth it. By directly stimulating the economy, government could rekindle demand and help reverse the downward spiral. Soon companies to invest again to increase production to ..owing demand. This would mean hiring ...ore workers who would soon have more money in their pockets. As jobs increased so would taxes, from workers and from businesses. Eventually, the government would be able to pay back its debt from increased tax revenues from a now healthy, growing economy.

Desperate Western governments were quick to adopt the 'Keynesian' solution to economic stagnation. In the US the 'New Deal' policies of the Roosevelt administration were directly influenced by Keynes. The American Employment Act of 1946 accepted the federal government's responsibility 'to promote maximum employment, production and purchasing power'. The British government, too, in 1944 accepted as one of its primary aims 'the maintenance of a high and stable level of employment after the war.'

Other countries, such as Canada, Australia and Sweden, quickly followed. Keynes' influence spread and people began to believe that economics was more than just the 'dismal science', a term coined by the 19th-century British historian Thomas Carlyle. Maybe it could actually be used to benefit human progress.

'We are witnessing a development under which the economic system ceases to lay down the law to society and the primacy of society over that system is secured.' Thus wrote Polanyi in a moment of supreme optimism just before the end of the War.

Bretton Woods

It was this confidence that delegates from 44 nations brought to the postcard-pretty resort village of Bretton Woods, New Hampshire, in July 1944. The aim of the UN Monetary and Financial Conference was to erect a new framework for the post-War global economy – a stable, co-operative international monetary system which would promote national sovereignty and prevent future financial crises. The purpose was not to bury capitalism but to save it. The main proposal was for a system of fixed exchange rates. In the light of the Depression of the previous decade, floating rates were now seen as inherently unstable and destructive of national development plans.

Keynes' influence at Bretton Woods was huge. But, despite his lobbying and cajoling, he did not win the day on every issue. The US opposed his 'soft' approach and in the end the enormous military and economic clout of the Americans proved impossible to overcome.

The Conference rejected his proposals to establish a world 'reserve currency' administered by a global central bank. Keynes believed this would have created a more stable and fairer world economy by automatically recycling trade surpluses to finance trade deficits. Both deficit and surplus nations would take responsibility for trade imbalances. However his solution did not fit the interests of the US, eager to take on the role of the world's economic powerhouse in the wake of World War Two. Instead the Conference opted for a system based on the free movement of goods, with the US dollar as the international currency. The dollar was linked to gold and the price of gold was fixed at $35 an ounce (28g). In effect the US dollar became 'as good as gold' and by this one act became the dominant currency of international exchange.

Three governing institutions emerged from the gathering to oversee and co-ordinate the global economy. These were not neutral economic mechanisms: they contained a powerful bias in favor of global competition and corporate enterprise. And each had a distinct role to play.

1 The International Monetary Fund (IMF)
The IMF was born with a mission: to create economic stability for a world which had just been through the

trauma of depression and the devastation of war. As originally conceived, it was supposed to 'facilitate the expansion and balanced growth of international trade' and 'to contribute to the promotion and maintenance of high levels of employment and real income'.

A major part of its job was to oversee a system of 'fixed' exchange rates. The aim was to stop countries from devaluing their national currencies to win a competitive edge over their neighbors – a defining feature of the economic chaos of the 1930s.

The Fund was also to promote currency 'convertibility' to encourage world trade – to make it easier to exchange one currency for another when trading across national borders.

And, finally, the new agency was to act as a 'lender of last resort', supplying emergency loans to countries that ran into short-term cash flow problems. Keynes' idea was to set up an International Clearing Union which would automatically provide unconditional loans to countries experiencing balance-of-payments problems. These loans would be issued 'no strings attached' with the purpose of supporting domestic demand and maintaining employment. Otherwise countries feeling the pinch would be forced to balance their deficit by cutting imports, lowering wages and dampening domestic demand in favor of exports.

Keynes argued that international trade was a two-way street and that the 'winners' (those countries in surplus) were as obliged as the 'losers' (those countries in deficit) to bring the system back to balance. Keynes suggested that pressure be brought to bear on surplus nations so they would be forced to increase their imports and recycle the surplus to deficit nations.

But Keynes did not prevail. Instead a proposal put forward by US Treasury Secretary Harry Dexter White became the basis for the IMF. The International Clearing Union idea disappeared. IMF members would not automatically receive loans when they fell into deficit. Instead members would have access to limited loan amounts which were to be determined by a complex quota system. Voting power within the IMF would be based on the level of financial contributions – one dollar, one vote – which meant that rich countries would call the shots.

When a country joins the IMF, it is assigned a quota which is calculated in Special Drawing Rights (SDRs), the Fund's own unit of account. Quotas are assigned according to a country's relative position in the world economy, which means that the most powerful economies have the most influence and clout. In 2009, for example, the US had the largest SDR quota at about 37.1 billion (about $59.3 billion) while the smallest member, Palau, had an SDR quota of 3.1 million (about $5.0 million). The size of a member's quota determines a lot, including how many votes it has in IMF deliberations and how much foreign exchange it has access to if it runs into choppy financial waters.

Nonetheless, the IMF was founded on the belief that collective action was necessary to stabilize the global economy just as nations needed to come together at the UN to stabilize the global political system.

The final decision was that balance-of-payments loans were to be contracted at less than the prevailing interest rate and members were supposed to use and repay them within five years. The issue of whether the IMF could attach conditions to these loans was unclear in the original Bretton Woods agreement. But Harry Dexter White was very clear six months later when he wrote in the journal *Foreign Affairs* that the Fund would not simply dole out money to debtor countries. The IMF would force countries to take measures which under the old gold standard (see p38) would have happened automatically.

The delegates at the Bretton Woods Conference supported a gradual reduction of trade barriers and tariffs. But they were less enthusiastic about allowing the free movement of capital internationally.

Keynes, Britain's delegate to the meeting, advocated a balanced world trade system with strict controls on the movement of capital across borders. He held that the free movement of all goods and capital, advocated most powerfully by the US delegation, would inevitably lead to inequalities and instabilities.

2 The World Bank (International Bank for Reconstruction and Development)

One of the other key goals of the Bretton Woods Conference was to find a way to rebuild the economies of those nations that had been devastated by World War Two. The International Bank for Reconstruction and Development (IBRD) was created to spearhead this effort. The Bank is funded by dues from its members and by money borrowed on international capital markets. It makes loans to members below rates available at commercial banks. Its initial mandate was to provide loans for 'infrastructure' which included things like power plants, dams, roads, airports, ports, agricultural development and education systems. The Bank poured money into reconstruction in Europe after World War Two. But it was not enough to satisfy the United States, whose booming industries were in need of markets. In response the US set up its own Marshall Plan, named after then US Secretary of State, George Marshall. From April 1948 to December 1951 the US provided $12.5 billion to 16 European nations, largely in the form of grants rather than loans.

As Europe gradually recovered, the IBRD turned from 'reconstruction' to 'development' in the newly independent countries of the Third World, where it became widely known as the World Bank. As Southern countries sought to enter the industrial age, the Bank became a major player. According to the 'stages of growth' economic theory popular at the time, developing nations could achieve economic 'take-off' only from a strong infrastructure 'runway'. It was part of the Bank's self-defined role to build this 'infrastructural capacity' and this it did enthusiastically by funding dams, hydroelectric projects and highway systems throughout Latin America, Asia and Africa.

But, despite the Bank's low lending rates, it was clear early on that the very poorest countries would have difficulty meeting loan repayments. So, in the late 1950s, the Bank was pressured into setting up the International Development Association (IDA). This wing of the Bank was to provide 'soft loans' with very low interest or none at all. It was not all altruism – it was also designed to head off Third World countries from setting up an independent aid agency under UN auspices, separate from the Bretton Woods institutions. In addition, the Bank established two other departments: the International Finance Corporation, which supports private-sector investment in Bank-approved projects, and the Multilateral Insurance Guarantee Agency, which provides risk insurance to

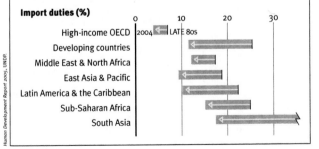

Tariffs are falling

In an effort to boost trade, developing countries have been leaders in reducing tariffs over the past two decades, often acting on their own with little outside pressure. The average tariff in the South fell from 25% in the late 1980s to 11% by 2004.

Import duties (%)

2004 ▨ LATE 80s

| | 0 | 10 | 20 | 30 |

High-income OECD
Developing countries
Middle East & North Africa
East Asia & Pacific
Latin America & the Caribbean
Sub-Saharan Africa
South Asia

Human Development Report 2005, UNDP.

foreign corporations and individuals who decide to invest in one of the Bank's member countries.

3 General Agreement on Tariffs and Trade (GATT)/ World Trade Organization (WTO)

Although Bretton Woods called for an International Trade Organization there was no consensus. The Americans balked at the idea that trade should be linked to employment policy or that Third World producers should get a fairer price for their commodity exports. So the General Agreement on Tariffs and Trade (GATT) emerged in 1947 to set rules on global trade in industrial goods only. Its aim was to reduce national trade barriers and to stop the beggar-thy-neighbor policies that had so hobbled the global economy prior to World War Two. After seven rounds of tariff negotiations over the next 40 years, GATT

The gold standard

Until the Great Depression of the 1930s gold was the one precious metal that most large trading countries in the world recognized and accepted as a universal medium of exchange. The shift to gold began when international trade exploded after the industrial revolution. Britain was the first to adopt the gold standard in 1816; the US made the change in 1873 and by 1900 most of the world had joined them.

Most national currencies were redeemable in gold. Paper bank notes often contained the phrase 'the bank promises to pay the bearer on demand' the equivalent in gold. That implied you could go into a bank and demand the equivalent in gold if the mood moved you.

What that meant was that all nations set the value of their national currency in terms of ounces of gold (1 ounce = 28g). It was a convenient way of settling national trading accounts. And the fixed gold standard was supposed to both stabilize foreign exchange rates and domestic economies. A country's wealth could be measured by the amount of gold it had stored in its vaults; certainly an unfair advantage for those countries lucky enough to be sitting on vast natural deposits of gold.

With gold as a fixed standard the fluctuations of international trade were relatively simple to track. If a country's imports exceeded its exports then gold had to be shipped to those countries who were owed in order to balance the books. The decline in the amount of gold would then force a government members reduced tariffs from 40-50 per cent to 4-5 per cent.

The final 'Uruguay Round' began in 1986. In March 1994, following its completion, politicians and bureaucrats met in Marrakech, Morocco, to approve a new World Trade Organization to replace the more loosely structured GATT. The WTO, unlike the GATT, has the official status of an international organization rather than a treaty. Unlike the Bank and the Fund, it does not set the rules. Instead it provides a forum for negotiations and then ensures that agreements are followed. By December 2009 there were nearly 150 member states, covering over 97 per cent of world trade, with 32 'observers' and over 30 others negotiating membership.

The WTO vastly expands GATT's mandate. The text of the WTO agreement had 26,000 pages: a hint

to reduce the amount of cash in circulation. Because money was redeemable for gold both governments and banks would want to make sure they could cover themselves if necessary. Less money in circulation would tend to lower prices, dampening economic activity at home and decreasing imports. Gold flowing to countries on the receiving end would have the opposite effect. Governments would release more cash into the economy to cover the increase of gold in their vaults and prices would tend to increase.

With the Depression of the 1930s one country after another abandoned the gold standard in an attempt to 'devalue' their currencies to gain a 'competitive advantage' over their trading partners (ie to make their exports cheaper). There was an attempt to modify the gold link after World War Two when the US set the value of the dollar at $1/35$ of an ounce (0.9g) of gold but holders of cash were no longer able to demand gold in exchange and the circulation of gold coins was prohibited. Then in 1973 US President Richard Nixon suspended the exchange of American gold for foreign-held dollars at fixed rates. At that point gold became just another commodity, its price determined by the law of supply and demand. Many countries (as well as the International Monetary Fund) continue to hold vast gold reserves and quantities are occasionally sold on the open market – though sellers are careful not to flood the market and depress the international price too much. ∎

of both its prolixity and its complexity. It includes the GATT agreements which mostly focus on trade in goods. But it also folds in the new General Agreement on Trade in Services (GATS), which potentially reduces barriers to investment in more than 160 areas – including basic needs like water, healthcare and education as well as telecommunications, banking and investment, transport and the environment. GATS is not a treaty. It's more like a framework agreement where negotiations can continue indefinitely. For large global corporations, it's a potential goldmine of new business opportunities.

From the outset GATT was seen as a 'rich man's club' dominated by Western industrial nations slow to concede their position of power. The WTO continues this tradition of rich-world domination. Rubens Ricupero, former Secretary-General of the UN Conference on Trade and Development (UNCTAD) is frank in his assessment of the multilateral trading system. It is a matter of 'concrete evidence', he said at the September 1999 G77 ('Group of 77' developing countries) Ministerial Meeting in Morocco, that global trade rules are 'highly imbalanced and biased against developing countries'. Why is it, asked Ricupero, that developed countries have been given decades to 'adjust' their economies to imports of agricultural products and textiles from the Third World when poor countries are pressured to open their borders immediately to Western banks and telecommunication companies? As a case in point, he mentioned the multifiber arrangement (MFA) on textiles under which industrial countries were allowed to impose quotas restricting clothing and textile imports from developing nations. The MFA developed from a waiver which the US demanded on behalf of its domestic cotton industry in the late 1950s. By the time the MFA was phased out in January 2005, it had lasted nearly 50 years – a long time for a 'temporary' concession which was to allow US producers to adjust to cheap textile imports.[1]

In contrast, according to the UN Development Programme (UNDP), developing countries have been much more willing to abandon import substitution policies and reduce trade barriers. The average tariff in developing countries fell from 25 per cent in the late 1980s to 11 per cent by the end of 2004. India, for example, reduced its tariffs from an average of 82 per cent in 1990 to 30 per cent by the end of 2004. Brazil chopped average tariffs from 25 per cent to 12 per cent over the same period and China lowered them from 43 per cent in 1993 to 18 per cent four years later. According to UNDP, only 79 per cent of exports from least developed countries were given duty-free access to the markets of developed countries in 2007. In addition, Organization for Economic Co-operation and Development (OECD) countries continued to subsidize their own agriculture to the tune of $363 billion in 2006 – almost four times the level of official foreign aid that year.

Notes UNDP: 'The world's highest trade barriers are erected against some of its poorest countries. On average, trade barriers faced by developing countries exporting to rich countries are three to four times higher than those faced by rich countries when they trade with each other.'[2]

Bananas rulings

The WTO pursues its free-trade agenda with the single-minded concentration of the true believer. Nonetheless, there is a growing unease about the organization's globalizing agenda. Critics are especially wary of the Dispute Resolution Body (DRB) which gives the WTO the legal tools to approve tough trade sanctions on a member-state, especially on nations that might disagree with the organization's interpretation of global trade rules. Any member country, acting on behalf of a business with an axe to grind, can challenge the laws and regulations of another country on the grounds that they violate WTO rules.

Previously, if GATT wanted to discipline one of its members for not playing according to the rules, every member had to agree. The WTO has considerably more power. The DRB appoints a panel of 'experts' which hears the case behind closed doors. If the panel decides on sanctions the only way to escape them is if they're opposed by every WTO member – a virtual impossibility. In effect, the WTO regime is one of trade über alles. Environmental laws, labor standards, human rights legislation, public health policies, cultural protection, food self-reliance or any other policies held to be in the 'national interest' can be attacked as unfair 'impediments' to free trade.

Already there have been cases where the WTO has effectively struck down national legislation in its pursuit of a 'level playing field'. The 1999 WTO decision against the European Union (EU) over importing bananas is a case in point. The WTO's 'most favored nation' clause demands that similar products from different member countries be treated equally. Under the terms of the Lomé Convention, the EU had promised to give preference to bananas from former European colonies in Africa, the Caribbean and the Pacific. In general, these banana growers tend to be small farmers who are less dependent on pesticide-intensive plantation methods than the giant US companies like Dole and Chiquita. Bananas account for about 60 per cent of export earnings in the Caribbean.

The Europeans stressed their right to determine a sovereign foreign policy in relation to former colonies while the US argued that EU tariffs prohibited American banana companies in Latin America from reaching lucrative markets in Europe. The WTO decided on behalf of the US, ruling that the European preference was unfair. Meanwhile, small island nations in the Caribbean, so dependent on income from the banana trade, are worried the decision will wipe out their major export market in Britain and destroy their industry. Quotas on the import of 'third country' (ie Latin American) bananas into the EU were finally eliminated in January 2006. (The Lomé Convention was replaced in June 2000 by the Cotonou Agreement, named after the town in Benin where the deal was signed.)

All nations have the right to use the DRB to pursue their economic self-interest. But the fact is that the world's major trading nations are also its most powerful economic actors. So the tendency is for the strong to use the new rules to dominate weaker countries. The 'national treatment clause' basically says that a country may not discriminate against products of foreign origin on any grounds whatsoever. And in so doing it removes the power of governments to develop economic policy which serves the moral, ethical or economic interests of their citizenry. WTO rules prohibit members from barring products if they disagree with the 'Processes and Methods of Production'. For example, if t-shirts or shoes are produced by children in sweatshop conditions that's irrelevant. The same is true if a foreign factory fouls the air, if poverty wages are paid to workers or if the goods themselves are poisonous and dangerous.

According to WTO rules, any country that refuses to import a product on the grounds that it may harm public health or damage the environment has to prove the case 'scientifically'. So Canada, the world's biggest asbestos producer, petitioned the WTO's dispute panel and won – forcing the EU to lift its ban on the import of the known carcinogen. And when the EU refused imports of hormone-fed beef from North America, the US took the case to the WTO, arguing that there was no threat to human health from cows fed on hormones. The EU ban on hormone-fed beef applied to their own farmers as well as foreign producers but that made little difference. The WTO panel decided in favor of the US, effectively ruling that Europeans had no right to pass laws that supported their opposition to hormones. The EU was ordered to compensate producers in the US and Canada for every year of lost export earnings. And in retaliation the WTO allowed the US to impose $116 million worth of sanctions on a range of European imports – including Dijon mustard, pork, truffles and Roquefort cheese.

Meanwhile, in 2001, the giant US-based shipping company, United Parcel Service (UPS), lodged a complaint with the North American Free Trade Agreement (NAFTA) – which runs a dispute resolution body similar to the WTO – threatening Canada's government-run postal service. UPS charged that Ottawa is unfairly subsidizing Canada Post and therefore poaching potential customers. In response, the Council of Canadians and the Canadian Union of Postal Workers (CUPW) asked Ontario's Superior Court of Justice to rule that NAFTA's investment rules are unconstitutional.

'UPS claims that, simply by having a public postal system, Canada is allowing unfair competition,' charged Council Chair Maude Barlow. 'By this logic, every public service from healthcare to education could face similar lawsuits. We don't intend to let foreign corporations destroy our public services.'

In June 2007, UPS lost its claim when the NAFTA tribunal hearing the challenge dismissed the $160 million suit against the Canadian government.

Meanwhile, in February 2006, the WTO ruled in favor of Canada, the US and Argentina in a dispute with the EU over genetically engineered crops. The WTO said that the EU discriminated against biotech seeds without adequate scientific evidence.

US agribusiness claims the ban costs American firms $300 million a year in sales to the EU. Critics, however, called the WTO decision a 'direct attack on democracy' – undaunted, EU governments had voted in 2005 to reaffirm their ban on GM seeds.[3]

And so it goes in the topsy-turvy world of economic globalization. Those institutions which first emerged from the Bretton Woods negotiations over half a century ago have become more important players with each passing decade. It is their vision and their agenda which continue to shape the direction of the global economy. Together, they are fostering a model of liberalized trade and investment which is heartily endorsed by the world's biggest banks and corporations. A deregulated, privatized, corporate-led free market is the answer to humanity's problems, they tell us. The proof, though, is not so easily found.

1 Martin Khor, 'WTO must correct imbalances against South', *Third World Network Features*, Oct 1999. **2** *Human Development Report 2005*, UNDP, New York, 2005. **3** 'Biotech industry gets boost', *Toronto Star*, 8 Feb 2006.

3 Debt and structural adjustment

Developing countries fight for a New International Economic Order, including fairer terms of trade, and push their case through UN agencies like UNCTAD and producer cartels like OPEC. Petrodollars flood Northern financial centers and President Nixon floats the dollar, sabotaging the Bretton Woods fixed exchange-rate system. When Third World debt expands, the IMF and World Bank step in to bail out debt-strapped nations. In return they must adopt 'structural adjustment' policies which favor cheap exports and spread poverty throughout the South.

THE GLOBAL ECONOMY has changed dramatically since 1980. So it's hard to believe that, only a decade before that, the newly emerging colonies of Africa and Asia were joining with the nominally independent nations of Latin America to push for a 'new international economic order' (NIEO). Throughout the 1960s and early 1970s, an insistent demand for radical change burst forth from the two-thirds of the world's people who lived outside the privileged circle of North America and western Europe. There was a strong movement to shake off the legacy of colonialism and to fight for a new global system based on economic justice between nations. Some Third World states began to explore ways of increasing their bargaining power with the industrialized countries in Europe and North America by taking advantage of their control over key resources. The Organization of Petroleum Exporting Countries (OPEC) was formed in the early 1970s, hoping to control the supply of petroleum and ratchet up the price of oil, thereby increasing their share of global wealth and bringing prosperity to their populations. OPEC's success led to heady talk of 'producer cartels' to raise the price of other exports like sugar, coffee, cocoa, tin and rubber so that poor countries dependent on one or two primary commodities could gain more income and control over their own development. There was also strong opposition to the growing power of Western-based corporations that were seen to be remaking the world in their own interests, trampling on the rights of weaker nations. When poor countries tried to increase the price of their primary exports they often found themselves confronting the near-monopoly control by big corporations of processing, distribution and marketing.

In the wake of OPEC, the NIEO was strongly endorsed at the Summit of Non-Aligned Nations in Algiers in September 1973. Then, in April 1974, the Sixth Special Session of the UN adopted the *Declaration and Program of Action of the New International Economic Order.* The following December the General Assembly approved the *Charter of Economic Rights and Duties of States.*

Key NIEO demands included:

- 'Indexing' developing country export prices to tie them to the rising prices of manufactured exports from the developed nations.
- Hiking official development assistance to 0.7 per cent of GNP of the developed countries (a target which has still not been met today).
- Lowering tariffs on manufactured exports from the developing countries.
- Transferring technology to developing countries and separating the process from direct capital investment.

Meanwhile, the *Charter of Economic Rights and Duties of States* endorsed:

- The sovereignty of each country over its natural resources and economic activities, including the right to nationalize foreign property.
- The right of countries dependent on a small range of primary exports to form producer cartels.

Debt and structural adjustment

The declaration of NIEO principles was the culmination of a new 'solidarity of the oppressed' which had spread throughout the developing nations.

Galvanized by centuries-old colonial injustices and sparked by the radical ideas of Frantz Fanon in Algeria, Kwame Nkrumah in Ghana, Mahatma Gandhi in India, Sukarno in Indonesia, Julius Nyerere in Tanzania and Fidel Castro in Cuba, these 'Third World' nations set out to collectively challenge the entrenched power of the United States and western Europe. The NIEO was not a grass-roots movement. It was a collection of intellectuals and politicians who believed that, left on their own, free markets would never reduce global inequalities. Instead these leaders argued for improved 'terms of trade' and a more just international economic system. When bargaining failed, producer countries began to form trade alliances based on specific commodities.

Third World nations also formed political organizations like the Non-Aligned Movement, which was initially an attempt to break out of the polarized East/West power struggle between the West and the Soviet Bloc. In the UN, developing countries formed the 'Group of 77', which was instrumental in creating the UN Conference on Trade and Development (UNCTAD). Within UNCTAD, poor countries pushed for fairer 'terms of trade'. Many newly independent countries in the South still relied heavily on the export of raw materials in the 1950s and 1960s. But there was a faltering effort and a stronger belief in the need to build local industrial capacities and to support the push for a new international economic order. Why was it that the price of imports from the West – whether manufactured goods, spare parts or foodstuffs – seemed to creep ever upwards while the prices for agricultural exports and raw materials remained the same – or even decreased? This patent injustice was one of the main concerns of the NIEO and the focus of its commodity program.

The plan was to intervene in the market, to regulate supplies and steady prices, to the benefit of both producers *and* consumers. The 10 core commodities were to be cocoa, coffee, tea, sugar, jute, cotton, rubber, hard fibers, copper and tin. This new commodity system was to be based on 'international buffer stocks' with a 'common fund' to purchase these stocks, as well as new multilateral trade commitments and improved 'compensatory financing' to stabilize export earnings. Unfortunately, the NIEO was never really given much of a chance by Western nations, who saw it as an erosion of their market advantage. Third World nations, meanwhile, were split by divergent interests and their lack of political power.

Transparent injustice

The transparent injustice of this enraged and frustrated leaders like Tanzania's Nyerere, who referred to declining terms of trade as constantly 'riding the downward escalator'. Between 1980 and 1991 alone, non-oil exporting developing countries lost nearly $290 billion due to decreasing prices for their primary commodity exports. In response to this economic discrimination, Third World nations also began agitating for an increase in 'untied' aid from the West; for more liberal terms on development loans; and for a quicker transfer of new manufacturing technologies from North to South.

In addition, most developing countries favored an active government role in running the national economy. They quite rightly feared that in a world of vast economic inequality they could easily be crushed between self-interested Western governments and their muscular business partners. That was the chief reason that many Third World nations began to take tentative steps to regulate foreign investment and to introduce minimal trade restrictions.

This process began in Latin America, where formal political decolonization had taken place much earlier, in the 19th century. Nations began to encourage 'import substitution' in the 1950s as a way of boosting local manufacturing, employment and income. Countries like Brazil and Argentina used a mix of taxation policy, tariffs and financial incentives to attract both foreign and domestic investment. US and European auto companies set up factories to take advantage of import barriers. The development goal was to stimulate industrialization in order to produce goods locally and to boost export earnings. This had the added benefit of reducing imports, which both cut the need for scarce foreign exchange and kept domestic capital circulating inside the country. Unfortunately, the era of import substitution was short. Latin American nations were soon bullied into dismantling import barriers – foreign-made goods, mostly American, soon flooded in again. Domestic industry took the hit. By the late 1980s, there were few local producers of cars, TVs, fridges or other major household goods. Still, this was a brief but important step in trying to shift the balance of global power to poor countries.

The petrodollar boom

Even before the clamor for a new world economic order, momentous changes were beginning to unfold that would dramatically alter the fate of poor nations for decades to come. By the late 1960s, the Bretton Woods dream of a stable monetary system – fixed exchange rates with the dollar as the only international currency – was collapsing under the strain of US trade and budgetary deficits.

As the US war in Vietnam escalated, the Federal Reserve in Washington pumped out millions of dollars to finance the conflict. The US economy was firing on all cylinders and beginning to overheat dangerously. Inflation edged upwards while foreign debt ballooned to pay for the war.

World Bank President Robert McNamara also leapt into the fray and contracted huge loans to the South during the 1970s – both for 'development' (defined as basic infrastructure to bring 'backward' economies into the market system) and to act as a bulwark against a perceived worldwide communist threat. The Bank's stake in the South increased five-fold over the decade.

At the same time, a guarded optimism took hold in the developing countries, fueled by moderately high growth rates and a short-term boom in the price of primary commodities, particularly oil. The Organization of Petroleum Exporting Countries (OPEC) was the first, and ultimately the most successful, Third World 'producer union'. By standing together and controlling the supply of oil, they were able to triple the price of petroleum to over $30 a barrel. The result was windfall surpluses for OPEC members – $310 billion for the period 1972-1977 alone. This 'oil shock' rippled through the global economy, triggering double-digit inflation and a massive currency 'recycling' problem.

What were OPEC nations to do with this vast new wealth of 'petrodollars'? Some of it they would spend on glittering new airports, power stations and other showcase mega-projects. But much of it eventually wound up as investment in Northern financial centers or deposited in Northern commercial banks. This was the birth of the 'eurocurrency' market – a huge pool of cash held outside the borders of the countries that originally issued the currency. The US dollar was the main 'eurocurrency' but there were also francs, guilders, marks and pounds.

Western banks, flush with this new OPEC money, began to search for borrowers. They didn't have to look for long. Soon millions in loans were contracted to non-oil-producing Third World governments desperate to pay escalating fuel bills and to fund ambitious development goals. At the same time the massive increase in oil prices helped inflation soar around the world. Prices skyrocketed while growth slowed to a crawl and a new word was added to the lexicon of economists: 'stagflation'.

In the midst of this economic chaos, US President Richard Nixon moved unilaterally to delink the dollar from gold. As a result the world moved to a system of floating exchange rates. Nixon also devalued the greenback (US dollar) against other major world currencies and jacked up interest rates to attract investment. Both moves had an enormous impact on the global economy.

By slashing the value of the dollar, Washington effectively reduced the huge debt it owed to the rest of the world. The US had been running a massive deficit to pay the costs of the war in Vietnam. As interest rates shot up, those countries reeling under

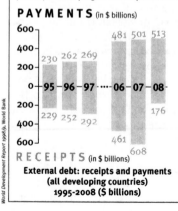

South pays North

Most of the increase in debt in recent years has been to pay interest on existing loans. It was not used for productive investment or to tackle poverty. Developing countries paid out more in debt service (interest plus repayments) than they received in new loans – a net transfer from the poor South to the rich North. This is likely to explode in the next decade if 2008 estimates in this graph hold. Preliminary data shows a 50 per cent reduction in net private capital flows to developing countries in 2008 and further reduction in 2009. Ironically, this 'reversal of international capital flows' eventually could be beneficial since private capital is often speculative and destabilizing. ∎

PAYMENTS (in $ billions)

95	96	97	06	07	08
230	262	269	481	501	513

RECEIPTS (in $ billions)

95	96	97	06	07	08
229	252	292	461	608	176

External debt: receipts and payments (all developing countries) 1995-2008 ($ billions)

World Development Report 1998/9, World Bank

OPEC oil-price hikes had the cost of their eurodollar loans (most of which were denominated in US dollars) double and even triple, almost overnight. The debt of the non-oil-producing Third World increased five-fold between 1973 and 1982, reaching a staggering $612 billion. The banks were desperate to lend to meet their interest obligations on deposits, so easy terms were the order of the day. Dictators who could exact payments from their cowering populations with relative ease must have seemed like a good bet for lenders looking for a secure return.

Sometimes the petrodollar loan money was squandered on grandiose and ill-considered projects. Sometimes it was simply filched – siphoned off by Third World élites into personal accounts in the same Northern banks that had made the original loans. Often it was both wasted and stolen.

Foolish loans
The experience was similar across the South. From the mid-1960s to the mid-1980s, despots were in power across Latin America and they employed an ingenious variety of scams. In Asia and Africa, too, megalomaniacs with powerful friends and large appetites for personal wealth were financed with enthusiasm by the international banking fraternity. Indeed, it seemed to work so well that the credit lines became almost limitless – particularly if the governments in question were fighting on the 'right' side of the Cold War and buying large quantities of armaments from Northern suppliers.

Examples of these foolish loans to corrupt leaders are well known. In the Philippines, the dictator Ferdinand Marcos with his wife, Imelda, and their cronies are estimated to have pocketed in the form of kickbacks and commissions a third of all loans to that country. Before he was forced out of office, Marcos' personal wealth was estimated at $10 billion.

Debt and structural adjustment

The Argentinean military dictatorship, famous for its 'dirty war' against so-called subversives, borrowed $40 billion from 1976 to 1983 and left no records for 80 per cent of the debt. Argentineans demanded that the Government either produce accounts or have the debts declared illegal. There is evidence that New York banks knew money was being misused, that there had been kickbacks and fraudulent loans to companies linked to the military, and that the IMF allegedly connived at the fraud. It is also clear that the military used some of the loans to buy weapons for the Falklands/Malvinas War. Then, in the 1990s, following IMF orthodoxy, President Carlos Menem privatized public services and industries and pegged

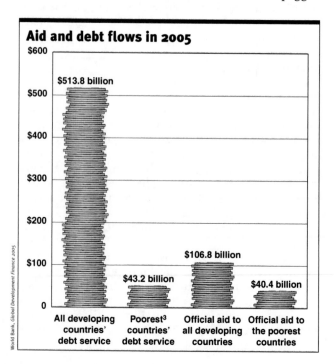

Aid and debt flows in 2005

- All developing countries' debt service: $513.8 billion
- Poorest[3] countries' debt service: $43.2 billion
- Official aid to all developing countries: $106.8 billion
- Official aid to the poorest countries: $40.4 billion

World Bank, Global Development Finance 2005

the Argentine peso to the US dollar. Finally, in early 2001, the whole edifice crashed. The crushing debt burden led to the complete collapse of the Argentinean economy. Bank accounts were frozen. The country defaulted on nearly half its $180-billion repayment obligations the following year and there was tremendous popular pressure to resist taking on further foreign debt.

Deeper in debt

From 1997 to 2000, the 'Jubilee 2000' citizens' movement led a worldwide campaign to cancel the debts of the world's poorest countries. The campaign attracted millions of supporters, North and South. Jubilee researchers found that almost a quarter of all Third World debt (then around $500 billion) was the result of loans used to prop up dictators in some 25 different countries – sometimes called 'odious debt'.[1] 'Odious', because citizens wondered why they should be obliged to repay loans contracted by corrupt governments who used the money to line their own pockets.

Loans flowed free and fast through the 1970s and early 1980s. But eventually the soaring tower of debt began to crack and sway. One government after another began to run into trouble. The loans they had squandered on daft projects or salted away in private bank accounts became so large that foreign-exchange earnings and tax revenues couldn't keep up with the payments.

During this period, the IMF became an enforcer of tough policy conditions on poor countries that were forced to apply for temporary balance-of-payments assistance. The loans were conditional on governments following the advice of Fund economists who had their own take on what Southern nations were doing wrong and how they could fix it. The demands were woven into the deals worked out with those countries that required an immediate transfusion of cash. Essentially, the IMF argued that the debtor country's problems were caused by 'excessive demand' in the domestic economy. Curiously, the responsibility of the private banks that made most of the dubious loans in the first place (with their eyes wide open, it should be noted) was ignored.

The IMF prescription

According to the Fund, this excessive demand meant there were too many imports and not enough exports. The solution was to devalue the currency and cut government spending. This was supposed to slow the economy and reduce domestic demand, gradually resulting in fewer imports, as well as more and cheaper exports. In time, the IMF argued, the balance-of-payments deficit would be eliminated. Countries were forced to adopt these austerity measures if they wanted to get the IMF 'seal of approval'. Without it they would be ostracized to the fringes of the global economy. As early as the 1970s, both the IMF and the World Bank

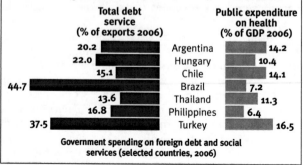

Creating poverty

In return for new loans to poor countries, lenders in the 1980s and 1990s insisted on 'structural adjustment' to increase their chances of being paid back. This meant cutting government spending on things like healthcare and education – the very services on which poor people (and women and children in particular) rely. Many of these countries have ended up spending more on servicing their debts than on the basic needs of their citizens. ■

Total debt service (% of exports 2006)		Public expenditure on health (% of GDP 2006)
20.2	Argentina	14.2
22.0	Hungary	10.4
15.1	Chile	14.1
44.7	Brazil	7.2
13.6	Thailand	11.3
16.8	Philippines	6.4
37.5	Turkey	16.5

Government spending on foreign debt and social services (selected countries, 2006)

Human Development Report 2008, UNDP, World Bank, www.worldbank.org

also urged debtor nations to take on deeper 'structural adjustment' measures. Initially, borrowing countries refused to go along with the advice.

Then, in 1982, when Mexico became the first indebted country to admit it could no longer meet its payments, a fully fledged Third World 'debt crisis' emerged. Northern politicians and bankers began to worry that the sheer volume of unpayable loans would undermine the world financial system. Panic began to spread as scores of Southern nations teetered on the brink of economic collapse. In response, both the Bank and the IMF hardened their line and began to demand major changes in the way debtor nations ran their domestic economies. Countries like Ghana were forced to impose tough adjustment conditions as early as 1983. A few years later, the US Treasury Secretary James Baker decided to formalize this new strategy to force Third World economies to radically 'restructure' their economies to meet their debt obligations. The 'Baker Plan' was introduced at the 1985 meeting of the World Bank and the IMF when both agencies were called on to impose more thorough 'adjustments' to the economic policies of debtor countries.

The Bank and the Fund made full use of this new leverage. Together they launched a policy to 'structurally adjust' the Third World by further deflating economies and demanding a withdrawal of government funding – not only from public enterprise but also from basic support of health, welfare and education. Exports to earn foreign exchange were privileged over basic necessities, food production and other goods for domestic use.[2]

The Fund set up its first 'formal' Structural Adjustment Facility in 1986. The World Bank, cajoled by its more doctrinaire sibling, soon followed – by 1989 the Bank had contracted adjustment loans to 75 per cent of the countries that already had similar IMF loans in place. The Bank's conditions both extended and reinforced the IMF prescription for financial 'liberalization' and open markets. They included 'privatizing' state-owned enterprises; reducing the size and cost of government through public sector layoffs; cutting basic social services and subsidies on essential foodstuffs; and reducing barriers to trade. This restructuring was highly successful from the point of view of the private banks, which siphoned off more than $178 billion from the Global South between 1984 and 1990 alone.[3] Structural-adjustment programs (SAPs) were an extremely effective mechanism for transforming private debt into public debt.

The 1980s were a 'lost decade' for much of the Third World. Growth stagnated and debt doubled to almost $1,500 billion by the decade's end. By 2002, it had reached nearly $2,500 billion. An ever-increasing proportion of this new debt was to service interest payments on the old debt, to keep money circulating and to keep the system up and running. Much of this debt had shifted from private banks to the IMF and the World Bank – even though the majority was still owed to rich country governments and Northern banks. The big difference was that the Fund and the Bank were always first in line, so paying them was a much more serious prospect.

Taking more out

The stark fact that the Fund and the Bank began operating with reverse capital flows (in other words they were then taking more money out of the Third World than they were putting back in) was sobering for those who believed those institutions were there to help.

In six of the eight years from 1990 to 1997 developing countries paid out more in debt service (interest plus repayments) than they received in new loans: a total transfer from South to North of $77 billion. Most of the increase was used to meet interest payments rather than for productive investment.[4] In 1998, the balance changed again as a result of massive bailout packages to Mexico and Asia. Nonetheless, figures for all private and public loans received by developing countries between 1998 and 2002 show that Southern nations repaid $217 billion more than they received in new loans over the same period.[5]

According to the Jubilee Debt Campaign the total debt of the very poorest countries (the 'low income countries' with an annual average income of less than $935 per person) was $222 billion in 2007. That same year, those countries paid over $12.4 billion to the rich world in debt service – $34 million a day. For all 'developing' countries, total external debt in 2007 was $3,400 billion on which they paid $540 billion in debt service. There was some debt cancellation in 2008 and 2009, but there were also massive new debts in response to the global financial crisis. As a result, the latest figures are bound to be even higher.

The 'conditionalities' of structural adjustment meanwhile diverted government revenues away from things like education and healthcare, towards debt repayment and the promotion of exports. This gave the World Bank and IMF a degree of control that even the most despotic of colonial regimes rarely achieved.

Even former 'economic shock-therapy' enforcers like Columbia University's Jeffrey Sachs were forced to reconsider their faith in this 'neoliberal' recipe for economic progress. In 1999, Sachs wrote that many of the world's poorest people live in countries 'whose governments have long since gone bankrupt under the weight of past credits from foreign governments, banks and agencies such as the World Bank and the IMF... Their debts should be canceled outright and the IMF sent home.'[6]

The situation has remained essentially unchanged ever since. In nations as far apart as former Yugoslavia, Rwanda and Peru, the privations suffered in the name of debt repayments lay concealed behind outbreaks of violent civil unrest. All attempts to organize relief for the South were rebuffed on principle until 1996, when the 'Heavily Indebted Poor Countries Initiative' (HIPC) was launched to make debt repayments 'sustainable'. But the HIPC initiative has a checkered history. In 2003, the 27 countries receiving HIPC relief still spent $2.8 billion on debt repayments, between 15 and 20 per cent of government revenues. The Jubilee Debt Campaign estimates that $400 billion of poor country debt is 'unpayable' – it is not possible for countries to pay it off while also providing health and education to their people. Most of these countries continue to spend more on debt service than on public health.[7]

Decades of structural adjustment failed to solve the debt crisis, caused untold suffering for millions of people and led to widening gaps between rich and poor. A 1999 study by the Washington-based group, Development Gap, looked at the impact of SAPs on more than 70 African and Asian countries during the early 1990s. The study concluded that the longer a country operates under structural adjustment, the worse its debt burden becomes. SAPs, Development Gap warned, 'are likely to push countries into a tragic circle of debt, adjustment, a weakened domestic economy, heightened vulnerability and greater debt.'[8]

Debt's legacy
So we are left with a bizarre and degrading spectacle. In Africa, external debt has more than quadrupled since the Bank and the IMF began managing national economies through structural adjustment. According to UN figures, Zambia has one of the highest rates of HIV/AIDS infection in the world, yet the southern African nation spends three times as much on debt service as it does on health. In Angola, where the average person lives to 42 years of age and 12 per cent of all babies die at birth, debt payments

are nearly five times greater than spending on health-care. In the late 1990s, half of all primary-school-age children in Africa were not in school yet governments spent four times more on debt payments than they spent on health and education. Sub-Saharan Africa has just 1.3 per cent of the world's trained health workers yet it paid more than $23 billion in debt payments in 2005.

In 2004, Ecuador spent 12 per cent of its GDP on debt service compared to 2.2 per cent on healthcare and 1 per cent on education. A year later, when a new government decided to direct oil money towards social spending, the IMF and World Bank balked. The Bank delayed and ultimately canceled an already approved loan as a result of what it described as a 'policy reversal'.

SAPs may not have put Third World countries back on a steady economic keel but they have certainly helped undermine democracy in those nations. Critics call it a new form of colonialism.

'Southern debt,' writes political scientist Susan George, 'has relatively little to do with money and finance, and everything to do with the West's continuing exercise of political and economic control. Just think of the advantages: no army, no costly colonial administration, rock-bottom prices for raw materials... It's a dream system and Western powers won't abandon it unless their own outraged citizens – or a far greater unity among debtor nations themselves – oblige them to so do.'[9]

Joseph Stiglitz, former World Bank Chief Economist, is candid about the record of bureaucrats in both the IMF and the World Bank who have eroded the ability of states to govern their own affairs. In an article written shortly after his resignation, Stiglitz said there are 'real risks associated with delegating excessive power to international agencies... The institution can actually become an interest group itself, concerned with maintaining its position and advancing its power.'[10]

Years later, he continued his attack on the limitations of 'market fundamentalism' preached by the IMF and the World Bank. 'The institutions are dominated not just by the wealthiest industrial countries but by the commercial and financial interests in those countries and the policies naturally reflect this... The institutions are not representative of the nations they serve.'[11]

Servicing the national debt has become a major concern in rich and poor countries alike. But especially so in the South, where there are far fewer dollars to spend: debt has become a major brake on development. In 2006, 52 developing countries spent more on debt service than on public health. Ten spent more on debt service than on education.

Dissenting voices

With the break-up of the Soviet Union and the boom times of the early years of the new millennium the triumph of capitalism seemed complete. But with the great financial meltdown that began in late 2007 that victory is no longer so certain. Nonetheless, memories are short. Deficit fetishism is on the rise, even as unemployment hits record levels. A quick 'jobless' recovery may derail the move for radical reform.

What is certain is that structural adjustment is an integral part of a globalized economy. Indeed, SAPs make sense when seen through the lens of an economic globalization that puts the economy ahead of people, rather than the other way round. This 'market fundamentalism' even has its own basic credo: the freedom of private corporations to trade, invest and move capital around the globe with a minimum amount of government interference.

But there are fault lines emerging in this élite consensus. People in the South are resisting structural adjustment through violent opposition and grassroots organizing. Protest too is coming from the millions uprooted by World Bank mega-projects, particularly the building of huge hydroelectric dams.

Opposition to free trade is on the rise. And in Latin America, governments opposed to the 'Washington Consensus' have been elected in Uruguay, Paraguay, Argentina, Brazil, Ecuador, Bolivia and Venezuela. The one-size-fits-all model of economic globalization is no longer accepted. Religious extremism and the politics of ethnic exclusion (from Palestine to Iraq to India) are turning political costs into military ones. And, as continuing protests against the World Trade Organization and the G8 prove, powerful and unaccountable institutions are coming under pressure from citizens' groups, community activists, students, trade unionists and environmentalists. Many are calling for reform. Others are going much farther and demanding the outright abolition of these agencies and a complete restructuring of the global economic system.

1 Joseph Hanlon, 'Take the hit!' New Internationalist, No 312, May 1999. 2 Economic Justice Report, Ecumenical Coalition for Economic Justice, Vol X, No 4, Dec 1999. 3 'How Bretton Woods re-ordered the world', New Internationalist, No 257, July 1994. 4 'Debt: the facts', New Internationalist, No 312, May 1999. 5 Eric Toussaint, Your Money or Your Life, Haymarket, Chicago, 2005. 6 The Independent, London, 1 Feb 1999. 7 Human Development Report 2005, UNDP, New York, 2005. 8 'Conditioning debt relief on adjustment: creating conditions for more indebtedness', Development Gap, Washington 1999. 9 Susan George, Another World Is Possible If..., Verso, London/New York, 2004. 10 Jim Lobe, 'Finance: Stiglitz calls for more open debate, less conditionality,' IPS, 30 Nov 1999. 11 Joseph Stiglitz, Globalization and its Discontents, Norton, New York/London, 2003.

4 The corporate century

Giant private companies have become the driving force behind economic globalization, wielding more power than many nation-states. Business values of 'efficiency' and 'competition' now dominate the debate on social policy, the public interest and the role of government. The tendency to monopoly, combined with decreasing rates of profit, drives and structures corporate decision-making – with little regard for the social, environmental and economic consequences of those decisions.

THE MOST JARRING aspects of travel today are not the cultural differences – though thankfully those still exist – but the commercial similarities. Increasingly, where we travel to feels more and more like the place we just left.

Whether it's Montreal or Mumbai, Beijing or Buenos Aires, globalization has introduced a level of commercial culture which is eerily homogenous. The glitzy, air-conditioned shopping malls are interchangeable; the same shops sell the same goods. Fast food restaurants like KFC, Burger King and Taco Bell all feature high-sugar, high-fat foods with minor concessions to local tastes. Young people use the same mobile phones, drink the same soft drinks, smoke the same cigarettes, wear identical branded clothing, play the same computer games, watch the same Hollywood films and listen to the same Western pop music.

Welcome to the world of the transnational corporation, a cultural and economic tsunami that is roaring across the globe and replacing the spectacular diversity of human society with a Westernized version of the good life. As corporations market the consumer dream of wealth and glamor, local cultures around the world are marginalized and devalued. Family and community bonds are disintegrating as social relationships are 'commodified' and reduced to what the English social critic Thomas Carlyle called the 'cash nexus' in his 1839 essay, *Chartism*. In the words of Swedish sociologist, Helena Norberg-Hodge, there is 'a global monoculture which is now able to disrupt traditional cultures with a shocking speed and finality and which surpasses anything the world has witnessed before.'[1]

Over the past two decades, as the global rules regulating the movement of goods and investment have been relaxed, private corporations have expanded their global reach so that their decisions now touch the lives of people in the most distant parts of the world. The vast, earth-straddling companies dominate global trade in everything from computers and pharmaceuticals to insurance, banking and cinema. Their holdings are so numerous and so Byzantine that it is often impossible to trace the chain of ownership. Even so, it is estimated that a third of all trade in the international economy results from shuffling goods between branches of the same corporation.

Some proponents of globalization argue that transnationals are the ambassadors of democracy. They insist that free markets and political freedoms are inextricably bound together and that the introduction of the first will inevitably lead to the second. Unfortunately, the facts don't support their claim. Market economies flourish in some of the world's most autocratic and tyrannical states and transnational corporations have shown surprisingly little interest in, and have had even less effect on, changing political systems. Saudi Arabia, Malaysia, Indonesia, Pakistan, China, Colombia: all have thriving market systems where transnational corporations are dominant actors. But none of them can be counted among the world's healthy democracies.

As the US political scientist Benjamin Barber has written: 'Capitalism requires consumers with access to markets and a stable political climate in order to succeed; such conditions may or may not be fostered by democracy, which can be disorderly and even anarchic in its early stages, and which often pursues public goods costly to or at odds with private market imperatives... capitalism does not need or entail democracy.'[2]

Many global corporations now wield more economic power than nation-states. According to one study by the Institute for Policy Studies nearly a decade ago, 133 of the world's 200 largest economies are corporations and only 67 are countries. General Motors was at that stage bigger than Denmark; Wal-Mart was bigger than Poland, South Africa or Greece; and Volkswagen was larger than Malaysia, Pakistan or Chile.[3]

The same study found:

- The world's top 200 corporations accounted for 25 per cent of global economic activity but employed less than one per cent of its workforce.
- Combined sales of the top 200 were 18 times more than the total annual income of 1.2 billion people living in absolute poverty – 24 per cent of the total world population.
- The profits of the top 200 grew 362.4 per cent from 1983 to 1999 while the number of people they employed grew by just 14.4 per cent.

Of course large companies have not just appeared on the scene. They've been with us since the early days of European expansion when governments routinely granted economic 'adventurers' like the Hudson Bay Company and the East India Company the right to control vast swaths of the planet in an attempt to consolidate imperial rule. But there has been nothing in history to match the economic muscle and political clout of today's giants – they grow larger and more powerful by the day. Scarcely a week goes by without another merger between major corporations. The global competition for market share over the past decade has been the catalyst for the biggest shift towards monopoly in the last century.

Consolidation has been particularly rapid in the telecommunications and media industries, where it is impossible to keep up with the endless mergers. A decade ago, what was then the world's biggest internet provider, America Online (AOL), announced a $160-billion merger with Time-Warner. The UK-based music giant EMI then unveiled plans for a $20-billion liaison with Time-Warner – creating the world's

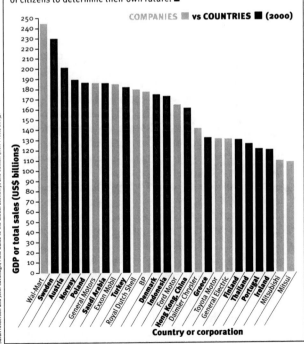

Corporate rule

Huge global corporations are becoming ever more powerful, eroding the regulatory powers of nation-states and riding roughshod over the rights of citizens to determine their own future. ■

COMPANIES ▨ vs COUNTRIES ■ (2000)

GDP or total sales (US$ billions)

Country or corporation

Wal-Mart, Sweden, Austria, Norway, Poland, General Motors, Saudi Arabia, Exxon Mobil, Turkey, Royal Dutch Shell, BP, Denmark, Indonesia, Ford Motor, Hong Kong, China, Daimler Chrysler, Greece, Toyota Motor, General Electric, Finland, Thailand, Portugal, Ireland, Mitsubishi, Mitsui

Sarah Anderson and John Cavanagh, *Field Guide to the Global Economy*, 2nd edition (New Press, 2005).

largest music firm. In the pharmaceutical sector in 2009, the US giant, Pfizer Inc, snapped up Wyeth for $64.48 billion while the German firm, Merck and Co, bought Schering Plough for $45.91 billion to become the world's second-largest drug company. Meanwhile, Germany's Daimler-Benz purchased Chrysler Motors for $43 billion while the Chinese company, Lenovo, bought the iconic computer giant IBM's personal computer division for $1.75 billion. In 2006, the governments of both France and Luxembourg fought a losing battle against the $34-billion hostile takeover of Arcelor SA by the world's biggest steel company, India-based Mittal. The merger created the world's first 100-million-ton-plus steel producer, with a market capitalization of $45 billion.

UN figures indicate that the tendency towards monopoly is growing across a range of industries, including manufacturing, banking and finance, media and entertainment, and communication technologies. But high-profile business marriages are also taking place in older industries like automobiles and transport as well as in primary resources such as mining, forestry and agriculture. The 10 largest corporations in their field now control 86 per cent of the telecommunications sector, 85 per cent of the pesticides industry, 70 per cent of the computer industry and 35 per cent of the pharmaceutical industry. Between 2003 and 2005, the world's top 10 seed companies increased their control of the world's global seed trade from one third to one half.

According to the accounting firm KPMG, the global mergers and acquisitions (M&As) market in 2005 involved 24,806 deals worth a combined $2,059 billion, a 19-per-cent leap over the previous year.

The recent economic crash curbed corporate merger mania: 2008 mergers fell by 30 per cent. But KPMG predicts a rebounding global economy will soon put M&As back on track. Stock markets reward the merged corporations with higher share prices on the grounds that the new larger firms will be more 'efficient' and therefore increase company earnings. But what does that notion of 'efficiency' really mean? Mergers squander vast amounts of resources for no productive purpose. The public impact of this very private decision-making process is rarely considered. When two corporate giants merge it inevitably leads to thousands of job losses and scores of factory closures. In fact this is precisely the point – to bolster the bottom line by trimming costs. When the UK companies Glaxo (now GlaxoSmithKline) and Wellcome merged, a tenth of the total workforce (7,500 workers) lost their jobs. Good news for shareholders, but not such good news if you were one of the workers who received your dismissal notice.

Merging businesses
Business executives champion the economic 'common sense' of mergers and push for their approval on the grounds that getting bigger is the only way to compete in a lean and mean global marketplace. But while size does matter in terms of a company's ability to compete, ironically a smaller number of large companies also heightens the tendency towards monopoly by eliminating competition. The easiest way to get rid of a competitor is to buy them out. Giant companies also have greater powers to wrest concessions from national and regional governments simply because they are such dominant economic players, creating jobs (albeit fewer of them) and boosting national income.

The spate of mergers and acquisitions over the last decade reflects the quickly changing nature of the global economy, especially the loosening of foreign investment regulations and the liberalization of international capital flows. Companies are now freer to compete globally, to grow and expand into overseas markets – and the recent shift to free trade in goods, services and investment capital is furthering this consolidation.

The assumption that competition is good 'in and of itself' is central to the corporate-led model of economic globalization. It's this belief that has led to a worldwide campaign by the economically powerful in favor of privatizing publicly owned enterprises. According to this conservative view, government must be downsized and its role in the provision of public services curtailed. The argument is that governments are inefficient bureaucracies that waste taxpayers' money – so they must be restrained. This criticism resonates to some extent with most people on the political spectrum, left and right. Perhaps that's why when right-wing critics began to bemoan the costs of big government in the 1970s it didn't take them long to find a sympathetic ear. But rather than strengthen the role of the state by streamlining bureaucratic inefficiencies and making government work better, they argued that private business should do the job instead.

This manic enthusiasm for privatization exploded when Margaret Thatcher came to power in Britain

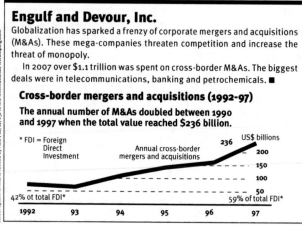

Engulf and Devour, Inc.

Globalization has sparked a frenzy of corporate mergers and acquisitions (M&As). These mega-companies threaten competition and increase the threat of monopoly.

In 2007 over $1.1 trillion was spent on cross-border M&As. The biggest deals were in telecommunications, banking and petrochemicals. ■

Cross-border mergers and acquisitions (1992-97)

The annual number of M&As doubled between 1990 and 1997 when the total value reached $236 billion.

* FDI = Foreign Direct Investment

Annual cross-border mergers and acquisitions

236 US$ billions

42% ot total FDI*   59% of total FDI*

1992 93 94 95 96 97

in 1979. State-owned enterprises were sold off: the national airline, government-run water, gas, telephone and electric utilities, and the railway system. From 1979 to 1994 the overall number of jobs in the public sector in the UK was reduced from seven million to five million. During the same period, the number of new jobs created by the private sector was minimal and the bulk of those jobs were in the non-unionized, low-paid, service sector. In the case of British Rail, the 1996 privatization created an inefficient, accident-prone system supported by massive public subsidies. After privatization, the number of canceled trains tripled while more than 2,000 contractors were involved in maintaining infrastructure.[4] For a one-off payment to the public purse, the UK Government sold state-owned enterprises that had contributed guaranteed, yearly profits to the Treasury.

While much was made of the opportunity for ordinary British people to buy shares in the newly privatized public utilities, the reality was quite different. Nine million UK residents did buy shares but most of them invested less than £1,000 and sold them quickly when they found they could turn a quick profit.

The majority of shares of the former publicly owned companies are now controlled by institutional investors and wealthy individuals. Susan George has called privatization 'the alienation and surrender of the product of decades of work by thousands of people to a tiny minority of large investors'.[5]

As governments adopt the private enterprise model and cut public expenditure, they open up areas to market forces that were previously considered the responsibility of the state. After World War Two, politicians in the West were forced by a civic-minded electorate to expand social welfare policies including education, healthcare, unemployment insurance, state pensions and other social security measures. At the same time the state expanded its role in the provision of public infrastructure, building roads, bridges, dams, airports, prisons and hospitals.

Now, with the notion of the 'inefficient' public sector firmly fixed in people's minds, governments are selling off public utilities like water, electricity and airports – often because operating budgets have been slashed to ribbons. Even prisons and parks are being privatized as governments pare public expenditure to meet market demands for balanced budgets. Make no mistake about it, these areas offer tremendous scope for private profits. In the US alone the total budget for prisons and jails in 1997 was more than $31 billion.

Privatizing healthcare
Other areas are also being eyed enthusiastically by the private sector. Take state-funded healthcare. In Canada, Australia and Europe private companies are making major inroads into publicly financed healthcare as deficit-conscious politicians slash budgets. This systematic de-funding may increase as governments once again target public debt after the current recession.

At the international level, the General Agreement on Trade in Services (GATS), administered by the World Trade Organization (WTO), was created in 1994. One of the goals of the GATS is to classify the public health sector as part of the 'service industry', eventually opening the door to full-scale commercialization along the lines of the US model where private corporations are dominant.

The for-profit health sector in the US has been actively lobbying to pave the way for their overseas expansion. A document by the US Coalition of Service Industries in November 1999 suggested that Washington push the WTO to 'encourage more privatization' and to provide 'market access and national treatment allowing provision of all healthcare services cross-border'. The ultimate goal was clearly spelled out: to allow 'majority foreign ownership of healthcare facilities'. The dry, technical language of the market is already infecting the debate around healthcare policy. But the great fear for those defending universal, state-funded healthcare is that privatization will lead to a two-tier system where wealthy patients pay for quick, high-tech care while the rest of us put up with poorly equipped, underfunded hospitals, long waiting lists and overworked doctors, nurses and technicians.

Privatization has been strongly endorsed by both the World Bank and the IMF and is a standard ingredient in any 'structural adjustment' prescription. It is based on the notion that governments really have no business in the marketplace and that the least government is the best government. Despite the convincing claims of its critics, the Bank remains wedded to privatization.

Its Private Sector Development Strategy released in February 2002 reinforces what the Bank calls 'policy-based lending to promote privatization'. The initiative seeks to expand the Bank's business-friendly division, the International Finance Corporation, whose role

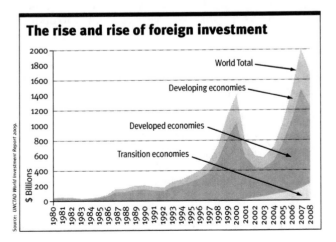

The rise and rise of foreign investment

World Total
Developing economies
Developed economies
Transition economies

$ Billions

Source: UNCTAD World Investment Report 2009.

is to open doors for private companies, both foreign and domestic. The emphasis is on increasing the role of private business in the service sector: water, sanitation, electricity, education and healthcare.

How much negotiating room do poor nations have to reject or shape adjustment policies which are presented to them by the Bank or the IMF as conditions of borrowing? The answer is virtually none. The right of governments (elected or otherwise) to make sovereign policy decisions on behalf of their citizens – a basic tenet of democracy – has effectively been jettisoned. The Bank and the IMF have been enforcing market fundamentalism for decades. Often privatization is a 'condition' for release of aid funds. To qualify for debt relief under the Bank's Heavily Indebted Poor Countries Initiative (HIPC), Southern nations are instructed to fall into line. According to an Oxfam UK report, debt relief to Honduras under HIPC was delayed for six months when the IMF demanded more progress on electricity privatization.[6]

Largely due to this arm-twisting, state assets have been auctioned off across the developing world and the former Soviet Union. In Russia, the transition to private ownership was riddled with corruption. Former Communist Party *apparatchiks* wound up in control of most state assets while billions hemorrhaged out of the country into numbered Swiss bank accounts. According to business writer Paul Klebnikov, the country suffered its worst economic decline since the Nazi invasion of 1942: 'There was a 42-per-cent decline in GDP. The population was impoverished. Mortality rates rocketed and the Russian State was essentially bankrupt.'[7]

Privatization in the South has been bedeviled by corruption, regulatory failure and corporate bullying. Take the energy sector. Often companies are reluctant to invest in power projects without a guaranteed return. Enter the 'power-purchase agreement' – a legal sleight-of-hand which requires a publicly owned electricity distributor to buy power from private producers at a fixed price in US dollars for up to 30 years – even if demand swoons and the power is not used. In India, the Maharashtra State Electricity Board (MSEB) was taken to the cleaners by the now-disgraced Enron Corporation and its $920-million Dabhol power plant. At one point, after renegotiating the power purchase deal, the MSEB was obliged to pay Enron $30 billion a year. Indian critics called the deal 'the most massive fraud in the country's history'. Indian novelist and activist Arundhati Roy says that the MSEB was forced to cut production from its own plants to buy power from Dabhol and hundreds of small industries had to close because they couldn't afford the expensive power. 'Privatization,' Roy writes, 'is presented as being the only alternative to an inefficient, corrupt state. In fact, it's not a choice at all... [it's a] mutually profitable business contract between the private company (preferably foreign) and the ruling élite of the Third World.'[8]

Attracting the money

In addition to selling off public assets, governments are constantly looking to attract private foreign investment. But investment by foreign corporations is by no means a guarantee of economic progress.

For example, a large part of foreign direct investment (FDI) is made up of companies buying out state firms, purchasing equity in local companies or financing mergers and acquisitions. Cross-border M&As account for about 80 per cent of total foreign direct investment yearly. Little of this ends up in new productive activity and there is almost always a net loss of jobs as a result of downsizing after mergers are completed. Increased investment from abroad can also cause a net drain on foreign exchange as transnational companies remit profits to their overseas headquarters.

If a foreign corporation produces mainly for local markets, and especially if it edges out local suppliers rather than replacing imports, it may significantly worsen balance of payments problems.

It's not the quantity of FDI that matters but the quality. National governments need to select the kinds of foreign investment that will produce net benefits for their citizens and reject those investments whose overall impact will be negative. Foreign investment can make a positive contribution to national development but only if it is channeled into productive rather than speculative activities. Unfortunately, the ability to shape foreign investment is dwindling as free-trade arrangements and bilateral trade agreements effectively tie the hands of states which agree to them, inevitably compromising government sovereignty.

Nonetheless, most Southern governments are anxious to attract investment from transnationals – despite the concern about corporate power and unethical behavior. With good reason – global companies are extremely skilled at delivering the goods. They are at the cutting edge of technological innovation and they can introduce new management and marketing strategies. And it's generally the case that wages and working conditions are better in foreign subsidiaries than in local companies.

But overseas investors don't automatically favor countries simply because they've loosened regulations on profit remittances or corporate taxes. The big money predictably goes to where it's safest and where the potential for profit is greatest. Most direct investment is concentrated in a small number of developing countries. According to UNCTAD's 2009 *World Investment Report* global FDI flows declined in 2008 and early 2009 'following a period of uninterrupted growth from 2003 to 2007'. Even though the share of developing and transition economies in global FDI flows surged to 43 per cent in 2008, the majority of investment in the South went to a handful of countries and the bulk went to just one country – China.

Transnationals are also major players in research and development (R&D). They account for close to half of global R&D expenditures and their spending can eclipse that of many countries. The world's largest R&D spenders are concentrated in a few industries – information technology hardware, the automotive industry, pharmaceuticals and biotechnology.

Draining the public purse

Investors crave stability, which is why nearly 60 per cent of all foreign investment goes to industrial countries. The US, UK, Germany, Australia, Belgium, France, Canada and Spain receive the lion's share. Yet even in the West corporations have the upper hand, trading off one nation against another to see who can offer the most lucrative investment incentives. Governments drain the public purse in their attempts to buy jobs from private investors. Tax holidays, interest-free loans, research grants, training schemes, unhindered profit remittances and publicly funded sewers, roads and utilities are among the mix of 'incentives' that companies now expect in return for opening up a new factory or office.

The largest transnationals call themselves 'global firms' which might lead one to believe that they are stateless, disembodied entities toiling for the good of humankind. The truth is more complex. There are few giant companies that are truly stateless; most are firmly tied to one national home base. Bill Gates' Microsoft is identifiably American, Total is French, Siemens is German, Vodafone is British and Nestlé is Swiss. These companies have no problem wrapping themselves in the national flag when it comes to lobbying local governments for tax breaks, start-up grants or other goodies. But at the same time their allegiances are fickle – and quickly diverted if opportunities for profit appear greater elsewhere. The fact that transnational corporations are relatively footloose means they can move to where costs are cheapest – and play off one government against another in the process. Examples fill the business press daily. Bombardier, a Canadian company that had received millions in government subsidies, announced in 2005 that it was exporting 500 highly paid, skilled jobs to India, China and Mexico, claiming that it needed to 'return to profitability by reducing operating costs'.[9] This political power – to pull up stakes, lay off workers and shift production elsewhere – is a powerful bargaining chip which business can use to wrest greater concessions from job-hungry governments.

One of the corporate sector's greatest political victories in recent decades has been to beat down corporate taxes. In Britain, the corporate tax rate fell from 52 per cent in 1979 to 30 per cent in 2000 and Prime Minister Tony Blair boasted that British business was subject to fewer strictures than corporations in the US. In 2010, the UK corporate tax rate was 28 per cent, below the US rate of 35 per cent and the French rate of 34 per cent but above Luxembourg, Iceland and Canada. Nonetheless, dozens of firms were planning to pull up stakes and move to Ireland where corporate taxes are a scanty 12.5 per cent.

Corporate tax rates have declined in virtually every OECD country over the last two decades as governments rely more and more on personal income taxes and sales taxes for revenues. In 1950 corporate taxes in the US accounted for 30 per cent of government funds; today they account for less than 12 per cent. In Canada, the effective corporate tax rate was cut from 28 per cent to 21 per cent from 2000 to 2004. By 2011 the effective rate will dip further to 16.5 per cent. Before the recent slump, corporate profits as a share of national income had hit an all-time high.

Their sheer size, wealth and power means that transnationals and the business sector in general have been able to structure the public debate on social issues and the role of government in a way that benefits their own interests. They have used their louder voices and political clout to build an effective propaganda machine and to boost what the Italian political theorist Antonio Gramsci called their 'cultural hegemony'. Through sophisticated public relations, media manipulation and friends in high places, the orthodoxy of corporate-led globalization has become the 'common sense' approach to running a country. This radical paradigm shift has occurred in the short space of 40 years – an extraordinary accomplishment by a cadre of right-wing thinktanks, radical entrepreneurs and their academic supporters.

Profits before people

The more our lives become entangled in the market the more the ideology of profit before people becomes accepted. A corporation's ultimate responsibility is not to society but to its shareholders, as Chief Executive Officers (CEOs) constantly reassure their investors at annual general meetings. Enhanced value for shareholders drives and structures corporate decision-making – without regard for the social, environmental and economic consequences of those decisions. The public is the loser. Unless social obligations are imposed on companies, the business agenda will continue to ride roughshod over national and community interests.

The North American Free Trade Agreement (NAFTA) was one of the first regional economic pacts developed to further corporate globalization. The Washington-based non-governmental organization, Public Citizen, has documented a steady movement of US companies to cheap labor zones in Mexico and the direct loss of hundreds of thousands of jobs since NAFTA came into effect in 1995.

The corporate century

The activist group cites the example of the jeans maker Guess? Inc which, according to the *Wall Street Journal*, cut the percentage of its clothes sewn in Los Angeles from 97 per cent prior to NAFTA to 35 per cent two years later. In that period the company relocated five sewing factories to Mexico and others to Peru and Chile. More than 1,000 workers in Los Angeles lost their jobs. According to the Washington-based Economic Policy Institute, the deal eliminated nearly 880,000 jobs, most in high-paying manufacturing, while the ones that replaced them were low-paid, non-unionized service jobs. NAFTA also had a negative effect on the wages of US workers whose jobs have not been relocated. They are now in direct competition with skilled, educated Mexican workers who work for a dollar or two an hour – or less. As a result their bargaining power with their employers has been substantially

---

Korten on corporations
Critic and author **David Korten** reflects on corporate power.

Corporations say the solution to poverty is to stimulate growth and create more wealth for everyone. Do you think that approach will work?
There is little evidence that economic growth alleviates poverty. Since 1950 the world's total economic output has increased five-fold while the number of people living in absolute poverty has doubled. This growth has pushed human demands on the eco-system beyond what the planet is capable of sustaining. And that does two things: it accelerates the rate of breakdown of the planet's ability to regenerate its natural systems. And it intensifies the competition between rich and poor for the resources that remain. I now believe that what the Gross National Product (GNP) really measures is the rate at which the economically powerful are expropriating the resources of the economically weak in order to convert them into products that quickly become the garbage of the rich.
Corporate leaders and their government backers claim free trade and open markets are the only way to have an efficient market system. Does business know best?
The modern corporation is specifically designed to concentrate economic power, and to protect the people who use that power from liability for the consequences of its uses. Free-trade agreements like NAFTA and GATT are not really trade agreements at all. They are

lessened. NAFTA was supposed to solve this problem by raising Mexican living standards and wages. Instead, both have plummeted, harming the economic prospects for workers on both sides of the border.

NAFTA's labor side-agreement was supposed to cushion workers but it didn't work out that way. Instead, labor protections built into Mexico's legal system have been attacked as obstacles to investment. In 2002, Mexican President Vicente Fox announced he would support the World Bank's recommendations to scrap most of Mexico's Federal Labor Law – eliminating mandatory severance pay and the 40-hour week. Mexico's historic (though not always enforced) ban on strike-breaking and guarantees of healthcare and housing would be gutted as well.

The policy of encouraging foreign investment at all cost also led to the wholesale privatization of Mexican

economic integration agreements intended to guarantee the rights of global corporations to move both goods and investments wherever they wish – free from public interference or accountability. Corporate power really lies in this ability to manipulate communities and markets in their own interest.

As corporations replace workers with technology they gain even more clout. Local governments are now forced not only to give them tax breaks but to subsidize directly their operations as well. This is what global competition is really about – communities and workers competing against each other to absorb even more of the production costs of the world's most powerful and profitable companies.

Is sustainable growth possible?

In my view 'green growth' is an oxymoron. In a deregulated market economy global corporations are accountable to only one master, a rogue financial system with one incessant demand – keep your stock price as high as possible by maximizing short-term returns. One way to do that is to shift as much of the cost of the corporation's operations as possible onto the community. The goal is to externalize costs and privatize gain.

A green corporation simply can't last in our unregulated market economy where competing companies are not internalizing their costs. If you do attempt to 'green' your business you'll soon be bought out by some corporate raiders who see an opportunity to externalize costs and make a short-term killing. ∎

Adapted from 'Development is a sham', *New Internationalist 278*, April 1996.

industry over the past decade and the effects have been devastating. While three-quarters of the workforce belonged to unions three decades ago, less than 30 per cent does today. Private owners reduced the membership of the railway workers' union from 90,000 to 36,000.

Since 1994, half a million Mexicans have been leaving their country every year. As the world crisis struck between April and June 2009, the economy shrank by more than 10 per cent; 700,000 jobs were lost from October 2008 to May 2009. In response, President Felipe Calderón prescribed a two-per-cent tax on food and medicine, together with sharp hikes in the price of electricity, gas and water

During the last two decades, the income of Mexican workers has lost 76 per cent of its purchasing power. Under pressure from foreign lenders, the Mexican government ended subsidies on the prices of basic necessities – including gasoline, electricity, bus fares, tortillas and milk – all of which have risen drastically. An estimated 40 million people live in poverty and 25 million in extreme poverty. Before the crash of 2007, the country's independent union federation, the National Union of Workers, claimed more than nine million people were out of work – a quarter of the workforce.

Well before NAFTA, the disparity between US and Mexican wages was growing. Mexican salaries were a third of those in the US in the 1970s. They are now less than an eighth. It is this disparity which both impoverishes Mexican workers and acts as a magnet drawing production from the US. By exacerbating these trends NAFTA forced working communities in Canada, the US and Mexico to ask some basic questions.[10]

The upper hand
As corporations gain the upper hand, fear of job losses and the resulting social devastation has created a

downward pressure on environmental standards and social programs – what critics of unregulated corporate power call 'a race to the bottom'.

Treaties like NAFTA, and new trade rules backed by the WTO, empower corporations while restricting national governments from interfering with the 'wisdom' of the market. But business is constantly pushing to expand the freedom to trade and invest, unhindered by either government regulations or social obligations.

The Multilateral Agreement on Investment (MAI) was one infamous example of the attempt by big business to remake the world in its image.

Public disillusionment with the WTO is well known. But if activists hadn't stumbled across the MAI in 1997, efforts to inject human values into the debate on the global trading system could have been severely curtailed. After the WTO was created in 1994, the globe's major corporations began to put together a plan for codifying the rules of world trade in a way that would give them complete freedom. They found it in the MAI, an agreement which was drafted by the International Chamber of Commerce (a 'professional association' of the world's largest companies) and presented to the rich-nation OECD members for discussion and, it was assumed, rubber-stamp approval.

Third World governments were rightly suspicious of the MAI and many saw it as 'a throwback to colonial-era economics'. But, with the weight of the OECD behind it, supporters of the MAI reckoned it would be speedily adopted as an official WTO document.

Delegates from OECD countries began discussing the MAI in early 1995 behind closed doors. By early 1997 most of the treaty was down on paper and the public was none the wiser. In fact, most politicians in the OECD's 29 member countries weren't even aware of the negotiations. When activists in Canada got their hands on a copy of the MAI and began sending it around the world via the internet the full scope of the document became clear.

Essentially the agreement set out to give private companies the same legal status as nation-states in all countries that were party to the Agreement. But, more importantly, it also laid out a clear set of rules so that corporations would be able to defend their new rights against the objections of sovereign governments. The MAI was so overwhelmingly biased towards the interests of transnationals that critics were quick to label it 'the corporate rule treaty'.

MAI protest

For example, under MAI provisions corporations could sue governments for passing laws that might reduce their potential profits. They could make their case in secret with no outside interest groups involved and the decision would be binding. The MAI also allowed foreign investors to challenge public funding of social programs as a distortion of free markets and the 'level playing field'. If a government chose to privatize a state-owned industry, it could no longer give preference to domestic buyers. In addition, governments would be forbidden to demand that foreign investment benefit local communities or the national economy. They could not demand domestic content, local hiring, affirmative action, technology transfer or anything else in return for allowing foreign companies to exploit publicly owned resources. And there were to be no limits on profit repatriation.

Once the text became public, citizens' groups around the world began vigorous education campaigns on the potentially damaging impact of the MAI. Two influential activists, Tony Clarke and Maude Barlow, summed up the feelings of citizens' groups everywhere. 'The MAI', they wrote, 'would provide foreign investors with new and substantive rights with which they could challenge government programs, policies and laws all over the world.'[11]

In a few months, public anxiety about the deal came to a head. In France, Australia, Canada and the US, politicians at all levels were drawn into the debate and governments were forced to enter 'reservations' to protect themselves from certain of the MAI's provisions. By the May 1998 deadline it was clear that the talks were at a standstill and that public opposition had torpedoed further progress on the Agreement.

This was a stunning victory for a growing international citizens' movement. But the end of the MAI as such did not spell the end of the corporate agenda for a global investment treaty. The focus would now shift to the WTO and other venues where transnationals could lobby for MAI-like investment provisions.

The downward pressure on wages and social programs caused by economic globalization is compounded by the rise of free trade zones (FTZs) which exist in dozens of Third World countries – there are now more than 1,000 FTZs operating, from Malaysia and the Philippines to El Salvador, Mexico and even socialist Cuba. These officially sanctioned sites exist almost as separate countries, offering their corporate clients minimal taxes, lax environmental regulations, cheap labor and low overheads.

Overcapacity
In their urgent effort to grow, corporations have ignored a fundamental aspect of capitalist production: over-capacity. It was Henry Ford, one of the pioneers of mass production, who realized 80 years ago the inherent dilemma of replacing labor with machines and then paying the remaining workers poverty-level wages. You could produce a lot of cars but in the end you would have no-one who could afford to buy them: too many goods and too few

buyers. Today, sophisticated improvements in manufacturing equipment have boosted productivity while
destroying millions of jobs and curbing wage growth.
Henry Ford's own automobile sector is a case in point.
One major reason for the massive restructuring in that
industry over the past decade is over-capacity, estimated at more than 30 per cent worldwide. According
to *The Economist* the global auto industry can produce
20 million more vehicles a year than the market can
absorb. And now low-cost Chinese automakers will
be joining the fray: the average manufacturing wage
in China is about 60 cents per hour versus $2.50 per
hour in Mexico. Unionized autoworkers in the US and
Canada make close to $30 an hour. The impact of the
global recession was a hammer blow to the US auto
industry as sales collapsed and iconic companies like
General Motors and Chrysler went bankrupt. There
may be just half a dozen major auto companies left
within a decade.

There is a global over-capacity in everything from
shoes and steel to clothing and electronic goods. One
estimate puts the excess manufacturing capacity in
China alone at more than 40 per cent. As industries consolidate to cut losses, factories are closed
but output remains the same or even increases. This
produces falling rates of profit, which in turn drives
industry to look for further efficiencies. One tack is to
continue to cut labor costs – which helps the bottom
line initially but actually dampens global demand
over time. Another is the merger and acquisition
route – cut costs by consolidating production, closing
factories and laying off workers. However, this too is
self-defeating in the long run since it also inevitably
reduces demand.

The real danger of this overproduction is 'deflation'. Instead of a steady rise in employment and
relatively stable prices for commodities and manufactured goods, deflation is a downward spiral of

both prices and wages. In economic terms, the logic is simple: productive capacity exceeds demand, prices fall, unemployment rises and wages are forced down farther.

In the 1930s, the result was a resounding and destructive economic crash which saw plants close and millions of workers made redundant. This catastrophe was reversed only when factories boosted production of armaments and other supplies for the Second World War. So far the specter of deflation has been kept at bay by making the US economy the 'consumer of last resort'. According to the IMF, the US has provided about half the growth in total world demand since 1988. The US may be reeling from the recent recession but the dollar is still vastly overvalued and its economy continues to suck in cheap imports from the rest of the world. Every day Americans borrow three billion dollars from foreigners – a form of 'vendor financing' – to pay for imports and to keep domestic interest rates low. The result is colossal domestic debt and record trade deficits. In 2008, as the economic crisis hit and imports fell, the US trade deficit shrank to $677 billion – down from $711 billion in 2007 but still 4.7 per cent of GDP. China's trade surplus with the United States increased from $11 billion in 1990 to a whopping $208 billion in 2009 – the country's largest bilateral deficit.

Fight for prosperity
In an era of globalized free markets, all countries try to fight their way to prosperity by boosting exports. That's partly because traditional Keynesian methods of stimulating domestic growth by 'priming the pump' had fallen into disfavor prior to the collapse of the global economy in 2007. And few countries have either the inclination or the political will to direct domestic savings toward investment in the local market. Instead, all nations look outwards; international trade is seen

as the only ticket to economic survival. The financial meltdown saw a dramatic turnaround in world trade. Manufactured exports worldwide fell by half or more from late 2007 to mid-2009, the first time world trade had contracted since 1945. A few years earlier, in 2004, according to the WTO, the value of world merchandise trade rose by 21 per cent to $8.88 trillion while trade in services jumped by 16 per cent to $2.10 trillion. Yet, as UNDP's 2005 *Human Development Report* points out: 'After more than two decades of rapid trade growth, high-income countries representing 15 per cent of the world's population still account for two-thirds of world exports – a modest decline from the position in 1980.'

The success of any country vis-à-vis another depends on how competitively (ie how cheaply) it can price its goods in the world market. This kind of competition inevitably means cutting costs and the easiest costs to cut are wages. But, as we have already seen, cheap labor exports inevitably backfire by undermining domestic purchasing power and depressing domestic demand. Simply put: workers earn less so they have less to spend. As University of Ottawa economist Michel Chossudovsky notes: 'The expansion of exports from developing countries is predicated on the contraction of internal purchasing power. Poverty is an input on the supply side.'[12]

Over the past 15 years, the UN has documented a steady shift of global income from wages to profits. Even so, investors are no longer satisfied with five or six per cent annual returns. Trade and investment barriers started to crumble as economic globalization took hold. But corporations, banks and other major investors were looking for quicker ways of maximizing their returns. The solution was at hand. From the 'real' economy of manufacturing and commodity production, investors turned to the world of international finance. Speculation and gambling in international money markets seemed easier than competing for fewer and fewer paying customers in the old goods and services economy. Welcome to the era of the 'global casino'.

1 Helena Norberg-Hodge 'The march of the monoculture', *The Ecologist*, Vol 29, No 2, May/Jun 1999. 2 Benjamin R Barber, *Jihad vs McWorld*, Ballantine Books, New York, 1995. 3 Sarah Anderson and Jon Cavanagh, *Top 200: The Rise of Corporate Global Power*, Institute for Policy Studies, Washington, 2000. 4 Brendan Martin, 'Derailed', *Multinational Monitor*, Jan/Feb 2002. 5 Susan George, 'A short history of neo-liberalism', paper presented to the conference on Economic sovereignty in a globalizing world, Bangkok, March 1999. 6 K Bayliss, 'Privatization and poverty', Jan 2002, http://idpm.man. ac.uk/crc/ 7 'The theft of the century', *Multinational Monitor*, Jan/Feb 2002. 8 Arundhati Roy, *Power politics*, South End Press, Boston, 2001. 9 '90 more Downsview plan jobs may flee', *The Toronto Star*, 27 Sep 2005. 10 Excerpted from David Bacon, 'Up for grabs', *New Internationalist*, No 374, Dec 2004. 11 This description of the battle against the MAI owes much to Tony Clarke and Maude Barlow, *MAI Round 2: new global and internal threats to Canadian sovereignty*, Stoddart, 1998. 12 Michel Chossudovsky, *The globalization of poverty*, Third World Network, 1997.

5 Global casino

The deregulation of global finance, coupled with the microelectronics revolution, has sparked a surge in the international flow of capital. This uncontrolled speculation has eclipsed long-term productive investment and poses a huge threat to the stability of the global economy. Recent financial crises, including the crash of 2007/08, caused suffering for millions and confirm the need for urgent action to control the money markets and rein in currency traders.

THE ACCELERATION OF economic globalization is dramatically altering life for people around the world. As wealth increases for a minority, disparities between rich and poor widen and the assault on our planet's natural resources speeds up.

But the biggest and most dangerous change over the past 30 years has been in the area of global finance. The volume of worldwide foreign exchange transactions has exploded as country after country has lowered barriers to foreign investment. In 1980, the daily average of foreign exchange trading totaled $80 billion. Today, it is estimated that more than $3,000 billion changes hands every day on global currency markets. That is about 50 times greater than the total value of all goods and services traded globally each year. An unimaginable sum of money.[1] But it is all the more stunning when you realize that most of this investment has virtually nothing to do with producing real goods or services for real people. Less than five per cent of all currency trading is linked to actual trade.

The world of international finance is technically arcane but the main point is easily understood. The goal is to make money – the end-use of the investment is relevant only to the extent that it is profitable. As growth in the real economy declines due to overcapacity and shrinking wages worldwide, speculative investment has grown. Money chasing money has eclipsed productive investment as the engine of the global economy.

There are very few controls on the movement of international capital. Yet the predominant view of the Bretton Woods institutions, the giant global banks and private corporations is that the world needs more financial liberalization, not less.

Others are not so sure. They're more inclined to believe what Keynes wrote in his 1936 book *The General Theory of Employment, Interest and Money*. 'Speculators may do no harm as bubbles on a steady stream of enterprise,' he warned, 'but the position is serious when enterprise becomes the bubble on a whirl-pool of speculation.'

The rules for running the global economy, laid down at Bretton Woods after World War Two, specifically sought to rein in finance capital and contain it within national borders. Keynes, Britain's delegate to the meeting, warned that unregulated flows of international capital would remove power from elected politicians and put it into the hands of the rich investors – whose ultimate allegiance was to their own self-interest.

Today that self-interest is creating havoc. Since governments in the industrialized countries began to deregulate financial markets in 1979, short-term specu-lation has become the single-largest component in the flow of international investment. Managers of billion-dollar hedge funds, mutual funds and pension plans move money in and out of countries at lightning speed based on fractional differences in exchange rates. This volatile flow of currency is almost completely detached from the physical economy. For every dollar that is needed to facilitate the trade in real goods, nine dollars is gambled in foreign-exchange markets.

Critics of corporate-led globalization charge that unregulated flows of capital pose a major threat to the stability of the world economy, turning it into a 'glo-bal financial casino'. This free flow of capital has also

had a direct political impact, leaving national governments hostage to market forces. Any departure from
the received wisdom is instantly punished. Without
regulation, investors can pull up stakes at a moment's
notice. Governments are hesitant to introduce laws
that might upset investors and cause capital to flee,
taking potential jobs with them and possibly sparking
economic chaos. This threat leads to a massive degree
of self-censorship and reduces the political space for
governments to control their own economic destiny.
That is the power of finance capital.

Currency speculation

The development of sophisticated computerized
communications combined with a global push for
further financial deregulation in the early 1980s to
open the doors to speculative investment. A decade
later, the World Bank, the IMF and the US Treasury
preached the benefits of liberal financial markets,
pressing Third World governments to open their stock
markets and financial services – banks, insurance
companies, bond dealers and the like.

As noted, the Bretton Woods agreements specifically
sought to limit the movement of finance capital and
contain it within national borders. Article VI of the
original IMF Articles of Agreement allows members
'to exercise such controls as are necessary to regulate
international capital movements'.

Under pressure from what Columbia University
economist, Jagdish Bhagwati, calls the 'Wall Street/
Treasury' complex, governments in the early 1980s
began to dismantle controls on both the flow of investment capital and profits across their borders. Bhagwati
argues that lax capital controls serve the 'self-interest'
of financiers by enlarging the area in which they can
make money.[2]

At the same time the financial services industry itself
underwent an unprecedented revolution, sparking a

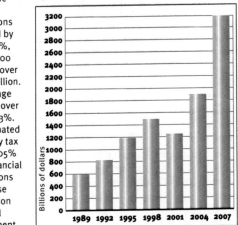

Riding the whirlpool
More than $3 trillion ($3,000 billion) changes hands daily on global currency markets.

- An estimated 95% of all forex deals are short-term speculation; more than 80% are completed in less than a week and 40% in less than two days.

- From 2004 to 2007 the volume of forex transactions increased by nearly 70%, from $1,900 billion to over $3,200 billion. The average daily turnover rose by 63%.

- It is estimated that a tiny tax of just 0.05% on all financial transactions could raise $400 billion for global development.

Rate of growth of foreign exchange markets

Figures for daily turnover in foreign exchange trading

Billions of dollars

1989 1992 1995 1998 2001 2004 2007

Triennial Central Bank Survey of Foreign Exchange and Derivatives Market Activity in 2007, Bank for International Settlements, www.bis.org

wave of mergers, acquisitions and overseas expansion. In most countries, banks, trust companies, insurance companies and investment brokerages were given the right to fight for each other's business and to compete across international borders. This level of deregulation had not been witnessed in Western countries since the Depression of the 1930s.

The growth in the finance industry was closely linked to the micro-electronics revolution. Computerization means currency traders can move millions of dollars around the world instantly with a few taps on a computer keyboard. Investors profit from minute fluctuations in the price of currencies. The result is what

Global casino

Filipino activist Walden Bello calls global arbitrage – a game 'where capital moves from one market to another, seeking profits... by taking advantage of interest-rate differentials, targeting gaps between nominal currency values and the "real" currency values, and short-selling in stocks – borrowing shares to artificially inflate share values, then selling.'[3] Volatility is central to this high-tech world of instant millions and Bello, among others, argues that it has become the driving force of the global capitalist system as a whole.

Besides speculating in foreign-exchange markets, money managers may also choose to put their funds into direct investment or portfolio investment. Foreign direct investment (FDI) – which tends to be stable and more long term – occurs when foreigners buy equity in local companies, purchase existing companies or actually start up a new factory or business. Foreign portfolio investment (FPI) – which is typically more volatile – is when foreigners buy shares in the local stock market. The trouble begins because portfolio investors have few ties to bind them to the countries in which their funds are invested. In the current global system, where liberalized financial markets are the norm, there are no constraints to prohibit investors from selling when they've turned a quick profit or exiting at the first signs of financial difficulties.

Portfolio investment
UNCTAD documented the shift from FDI to FPI during the 1990s. According to their 1998 *World Investment Report*, FPI accounted for a third of all private investment in developing countries from 1990 to 1997. And in some countries, like Argentina, Brazil, Mexico, Thailand and South Korea, portfolio investment actually outstripped direct investment. The UN agency notes that increasing FPI can signal a more volatile global economy because portfolio investors are 'attracted not so much by the prospect of long-

term growth as by the prospect of immediate gain'. Thus they are prone to herd behavior which can lead to 'massive withdrawals' in a crisis.

And there have been plenty such crises. One 2002 study from the US National Bureau of Economic Research found that there were 48 financial crises around the world from 1949 to 1971 and 139 from 1973 to 1997 in the era of hyper-deregulation. Since the 1997 meltdown in Asia, there have been financial crises in Russia, Brazil, Turkey and Argentina. And of course, the global crash of 2007/08 was the mother of all crises. All of them required active intervention by international financial institutions and national governments to keep the world system from collapsing. During the most recent financial debacle, governments around the world pumped more than $15 trillion into the global economic system, bailing out banks, ailing car companies, insolvent insurance firms and providing Keynesian-style fiscal stimulus packages to boost economic growth.

The 1997 Southeast Asian crisis was an early wake-up call. 'Hot money' panicked and fled as quickly as it had arrived. Although the IMF and the US government eventually stepped in with an emergency bailout of more than $120 billion, the damage was widespread. Currencies were devalued in Thailand, Indonesia, the Philippines and South Korea; factories were shut down, imports slashed, workers laid off and public-sector services like healthcare, education and transport cut drastically.

As the UN Development Programme commented in its 1999 *Human Development Report*: 'The East Asian crisis is not an isolated accident, it is a symptom of general weakness in global capital markets.' The UN agency was not alone in its assessment. Even the probusiness magazine, *The Economist*, admitted that abrupt reversals in capital 'have challenged the conventional wisdom that it is a good thing to let capital move freely across borders'. Others like Bhagwati were less equivocal. 'The Asian crisis cannot be separated from excessive borrowings of foreign short-term capital... It has become apparent that crises attendant on capital mobility cannot be ignored.'

The Southeast Asian economy went into freefall in the summer of 1997. In the 18 months prior to the crash more short-term investment had entered the region than in the previous 10 years. Capital flows into Thailand and Malaysia in the 1990s amounted to more than 10 per cent of Gross Domestic Product (GDP) and most of that speculative cash went into short-term debt. Previously, these nations had been more cautious about foreign investment and had taken steps to develop domestic industry by closing the door to cheaper imports from the West.

All that changed in the 1990s when these Southeast Asian countries became star pupils of the so-called 'Washington Consensus'. Both the IMF and the World Bank had advised the countries to deregulate their capital accounts as a way of enticing foreign investment and kick-starting the development process. Around 1990 Thailand, Malaysia, Indonesia and the Philippines all adopted an open-door policy to foreign investment. Measures included jacking up domestic interest rates to attract portfolio investment and pegging the national currency to the dollar to ensure that foreign investors wouldn't get hit in case of sudden shifts in the value of the currency.

Hot money

In one of the most thorough examinations of the impact of 'hot money' on national economies, Walden Bello outlines the case of Thailand. In 1994 the World Bank noted in its annual report that 'Thailand provides an excellent example of the dividends to be obtained through outward orientation, receptivity to foreign investment and a market-friendly philosophy backed up by conservative macro-economic management and cautious external borrowing policies.'

Ironically, it was in Thailand that the economic boom first began to fizzle – sparked by the herd mentality of short-term investors. In 1992-93 the country gave in to IMF pressure and adopted a radical deregulation of its financial system.[4] Measures included: fewer constraints on the portfolio management of financial institutions and commercial banks; looser rules on the expansion of banks and financial institutions; dismantling of foreign exchange controls; and the establishment of the Bangkok International Banking Facility (BIBF). The BIBF was a way for both local and foreign banks to take part in offshore and onshore lending. Firms licensed by the BIBF could both accept deposits and make loans in foreign currencies, to residents and non-residents. Most of the foreign capital entering the country soon came in the form of BIBF dollar loans.

The capital that flooded into Thailand was neither patient nor rooted. Most of it was invested not in goods-producing industries but in areas where profits were reckoned to be sizable and quick. Millions poured into the stock market (which inflated prices beyond the value of their real worth) and into real estate and various kinds of easy consumer credit like car financing. By late 1996 there was an estimated $24 billion in 'hot money' in Bangkok alone. As a result of this offshore investment, the country's foreign debt ballooned from $21 billion in 1988 to $89 billion in 1996. The vast majority of this – more than 80 per cent – was owed to the private sector.[5]

It was a similar story throughout the region. South Korea's foreign debt nearly tripled from $44 billion to $120 billion from 1993 to 1997 – about 70 per cent of that was in short-term, easily withdrawn funds. In Indonesia, companies outside the financial sector built up $40 billion in debt by the middle of 1997, 87 per cent of which was short-term. According to official figures the five countries in the region (Indonesia, Thailand, Malaysia, the Philippines and South Korea) had a combined debt to foreign banks of $274 billion just before the crisis: 64 per cent of that was in short-term obligations. This was a recipe for financial disaster.

Much of the speculative capital in Thailand went into real estate, always a favorite for those with a get-rich-quick dream in mind. So much money was pumped into Thai real estate that the value of unsold office buildings and apartments in the country nudged $20 billion. It was this massive bubble that finally frayed the nerves of foreign investors. When they woke up to the fact that most of their money was tied up in property, for which there were no buyers, and that Thai banks were carrying billions in bad debt that could not be serviced, investors panicked and hurried to withdraw their funds. The anxiety (later dubbed the 'contagion effect') spread quickly from Thailand and Malaysia to Indonesia, the Philippines and South Korea. Like the plague in medieval Europe, this financial chaos was felt to be a contagious disease that could jump national borders.

In just over a year there was a complete turnaround in the capital account of the region: in 1996, new financial inflows to the five countries totaled $93 billion. In 1997, $105 billion left those same countries – a net outflow of $12 billion. All investors rushed for the exit at the same time because none of them wanted to get caught with depreciated local currency and assets.[6]

Downward spiral

The vicious downward spiral picked up speed – egged on by speculators who intervened massively in foreign exchange markets and helped to seriously devalue local currencies. Under speculative attack, the governments of the region did what they could to ward off the inevitable. The first line of defense was to raid their own foreign exchange reserves to buy up their national currency in a last-ditch attempt to maintain its value. Under pressure from speculators, the Bank of Thailand lost almost all its $38.7 billion in foreign exchange holdings in just six months. But to no avail. Speculators continued to bail out in droves. The next step was to float their currencies but that too backfired, proving a catalyst for further devaluation. The Thai *baht* lost half its value in a few months. So the hemorrhage of foreign funds helped both to deplete foreign exchange reserves and to drive down the value of domestic currencies.

The *baht* felt the pressure first but the devaluation soon spread to the other countries. As the currency drifted downwards, local firms that had borrowed from abroad had to pay more in local currency for the foreign exchange needed to service their overseas debts. At the first sign that things were spinning out of control, many foreign banks and other creditors refused to roll over their loans. They demanded immediate repayment. At this point the panic that gripped the region suddenly became a crisis threatening to capsize the entire global economy. Soon, international financial operators were selling *baht*, *ringgit* and *rupiah* in an effort to cut potential losses and get their funds safely back to Europe and the US. In the ensuing capital flight, Asian stock prices plunged and the value of local currencies collapsed. Businesses that had taken out dollar-denominated loans couldn't afford the dollar payments to Western creditors.

For a time, governments tried to stave off default by lending some of their foreign currency reserves to the indebted private companies. South Korea used up some $30 billion in this way. But the money soon ran out and Western banks refused to make new loans or to roll over old debts. Asian businesses defaulted, cutting output and laying off workers. As the region's economies sputtered, panic intensified. Asian currencies lost 35 to

85 per cent of their foreign-exchange value, driving up prices on imported goods and pushing down the standard of living. Businesses large and small were driven to bankruptcy by the sudden drying up of credit; within a year, millions of workers had lost their jobs while the prices of imports, including basic foodstuffs, soared.

In an effort to calm investors and forestall total financial collapse the International Monetary Fund (IMF) introduced a $120-billion bailout plan. But the IMF rescue package actually succeeded in making a bad situation worse – not least for the citizens of those nations who had to endure the impact of the Fund's loan conditions. One of the central requirements of the package was that governments guarantee continued debt service to the private sector in return for the agency persuading creditors to roll over or restructure their loans. This mirrored the IMF's role during the Third World debt crisis of the 1980s. Public money from Northern taxpayers (via the Fund) was handed over to indebted governments, then recycled to commercial banks in the South to pay off their debts to private investors. In Asia some critics dubbed this bailout of international creditors 'socialism for the global financial élite'.

The Fund's Asian package also forced countries to further liberalize their capital account. The goal was to cut government expenditure and produce a surplus. The standard tools were applied: high interest rates combined with cuts to both government expenditures and subsidies to basics like food, fuel and transport. The high interest rates were supposed to be the bait to lure back foreign capital so all would be well again. But the bait didn't work. Tight domestic credit combined with high interest rates sparked a much sharper recession than would have otherwise taken place and did nothing to restore investor confidence.

Output in some countries fell 16 per cent or more, unemployment soared and wages nose-dived. In

Thailand, GDP growth-rate estimates plummeted after the IMF intervention, from 2.5 per cent in August 1997 to minus 3.5 per cent in February 1998. In Indonesia, the IMF forced the government to close down 16 banks, a move it thought would restore confidence in the notoriously inefficient banking system. Instead it led to panic withdrawals by customers at the remaining banks, which brought further chaos. It is estimated that half the businesses in the country went bankrupt.

The setback was so severe that non-governmental organizations estimated it would take a decade or longer to make up the lost ground. Oxfam analyzed the situation as follows: 'The crisis now gripping East Asia bears comparison in terms of its destructive impact with the Great Depression of 1929. What started as a financial crisis has been allowed to develop into a full-fledged social and economic crisis, with devastating consequences for human development. Previously rising incomes have been reversed and unemployment and underemployment have reached alarming levels. Rising food prices and falling social spending have further aggravated the social conditions of the poorest.'[7]

The impact on the region was stunning. According to the International Labour Organization (ILO) more than 20 million people in Indonesia were laid off from September 1997 to September 1998. UNICEF said that 250,000 clinics had closed and predicted that infant mortality would jump by 30 per cent. The Asian Development Bank said that more than six million children had dropped out of school. And Oxfam estimated that over 100 million Indonesians were living in poverty a year after the crisis – four times more than two years earlier.

There was also a frightening resurgence of racial 'scapegoating' and inter-communal violence throughout the region. Malaysia's leader at the time, the autocratic Mahathir Mohamad, blamed Jewish financiers for destabilizing his Muslim country, while

Global casino

in Indonesia the shops of ethnic-Chinese merchants were looted and burned and hundreds of Chinese brutally beaten and killed.

There were, however, some clear winners that emerged from the Asian meltdown. The big ones were the Western corporate interests that rushed in to snap up the region's bargain-basement assets after the economic collapse. As former US Trade Representative Mickey Kantor said at the time, the recession in the 'Tiger Economies' was a golden chance for the West to reassert its commercial interests. 'When countries

---

Market buzz

A pocket guide to the language of the financial market place.

• **Hedging**

If a business holds stocks of a commodity like cocoa or copper it runs the risk of losing money if the price falls before it can unload it all. This loss can be avoided by 'hedging' the risk. This involves selling the item before the purchaser actually wants it – ie for delivery at an agreed price at a future date. Hedge funds make a business of selling and buying this risk, often using borrowed money to put together 'highly leveraged' deals. The most infamous hedge fund, the US firm Long Term Capital Management (LTCM), had to be rescued with a $3.5 billion bailout from other Wall Street investment companies after it overextended itself to the tune of $200 billion. The firm had invested $500 million of borrowed money for every million dollars it invested of its own cash.

• **Futures, options and swaps**

A futures contract is an agreement to buy or sell a commodity or shares or currency at a future date at a price decided when the contract is first agreed. An option is like a futures contract except that in this case there is a right, but no obligation, to trade at an agreed price at a future date. An interest-rate swap is a transaction by which financial institutions change the form of their assets or debts. Swaps can be between fixed and floating rate debt, or between debt in different currencies.

• **Derivatives**

A sweeping, catchall term used to refer to a range of extremely complex and obscure financial arrangements. Futures contracts, futures on stock market indices, options and swaps are all derivatives. In general, derivatives are tradable securities whose value is 'derived' (thus the name) from some underlying instrument which may be a stock, bond, commodity or currency. They can be used as a hedge to reduce risks or for speculation. According to the Bank for International Settlements the

seek help from the IMF,' he said, 'Europe and America should use the IMF as a battering ram to gain advantage.'[8]

South Korea and Malaysia

That was certainly true in South Korea, where the IMF agreement lifted restrictions on outside ownership so that foreigners could purchase up to 55 per cent of Korean companies and 100 per cent of Korean banks. Years of effort by the Korean élite to keep businesses firmly under control of state-supported conglomerates

---

notional value of all derivatives in effect in June 2007 was $516 trillion, which dwarfs the value of all the world's stock markets combined.

- **Stock market indices**

The most famous are the Dow Jones Industrial Average, an index of share prices on the US stock market based on 30 leading US companies, the FTSE 100, an index of Britain's 100 top companies and the Japanese equivalent, the NIKKEI 225.

- **Foreign exchange market**

This is where currencies are traded. There is no single location for this market since it operates via computer and telephone connections in an interlaced web linking hundreds of trading points all over the world. The total turnover of world foreign exchange markets is enormous, many times the total international trade in goods and services.

- **Mutual funds/Unit trusts**

A financial institution which holds shares on behalf of investors. The investors buy shares or 'units' in the fund, which uses their money to buy shares in a range of companies. An investor selling back the units gets the proceeds of selling a fraction of the fund's total portfolio rather than just shares in one or two companies.

- **Equities**

The ordinary shares or common stock of companies. The owners of these shares are entitled to the residual profits of companies after all claims of creditors, debenture holders and preference shareholders have been satisfied. These are paid out to stock owners in the form of dividends.

- **Junk bonds**

Bonds issued on very doubtful security by firms where there is serious doubt as to whether interest and redemption payments will actually be made. Because these bonds are so risky, lenders are only prepared to hold them if promised returns are high enough. ■

called *chaebols* were undone in a matter of months. In January 1998, the French investment firm Crédit Lyonnais estimated that just 87 of the country's 653 non-financial firms were safe from foreign buyers. The US economist, Rudi Dornbusch, accurately summed up the overall impact of the economic slump: 'Korea is now owned and operated by our Treasury. That's the positive side of this crisis.'[9]

A key reason why the Asian economies were so vulnerable to currency destabilization was that they had gradually abandoned controls over the movement of capital. When a country cedes control over capital flows, it effectively removes any tools it may have for intervening in the market process, leaving itself at the mercy of speculators whose only concern is profit. More critically, nations lose the ability to control internal economic strategies which lie at the heart of national sovereignty. How can a nation hope to determine its own social agenda and economic future if key policy areas are shaped by the self-interest of foreign investors and money markets?

At the time of the Asian meltdown, one country emerged from the chaos in noticeably better shape than the others. Although Malaysia's GDP fell by 7.5 per cent in 1998, the nation managed to escape the devastating social impact felt elsewhere. Partly this was because Malaysia adopted a range of defensive measures to limit capital flight, many of which were modeled on the Chinese example.

The Malaysian Central Bank ruled that private companies could only contract foreign loans if they could show that the loans would end up producing foreign exchange which then could be used to service the debt. And like China, Malaysia also pegged its currency, the *ringgit*, to the US dollar and allowed it to be freely converted to other foreign currencies for trade and direct investment. Critically, portfolio investors had to keep their funds inside Malaysia for a minimum of one year and the amount of money residents could take out of the country was restricted.

Most important, trade in *ringgit* outside the country was not recognized by the government and this helped to prevent manipulation by currency speculators. Measures were also taken to reduce foreign investment in the Malaysian stock market. The controls allowed the government to stimulate the domestic economy with tax cuts, lower interest rates and spending on public infrastructure – without having to worry about speculators targeting its currency. Interest rates fell from 11 to 7 per cent, a helpful boon to local businesses and the domestic banking industry.

China, Chile and Brazil

Despite its authoritarian political structure China was also able to sidestep the Asian trap – mainly by avoiding becoming entangled in international financial markets. At the time of the Asian financial crisis, China had considerably more control over its domestic economy than just about any nation in the world. Its currency, the *renmimbi*, was not freely convertible; its finance system was owned and controlled by the state and there was relatively little foreign investment in the Chinese stock market. Plus the world's biggest nation was not then a member of the WTO – the country did not become a full member of the organization until December 2001.

As a result, China was not vulnerable to the speculative herd behavior that devastated other countries in the region. Instead of devaluing its currency and trying to grab a share of its neighbors' exports, China took another tack. The government decided to direct national savings into a $200-billion public works program to stimulate its domestic economy.[10]

Chile is another country that successfully tried to regulate destabilizing short-term flows of foreign capital by installing a series of financial 'speed bumps' to slow down speculation. When Mexico's economy crashed in 1995 Chile was able to escape the worst 'contagion' effects because of its *encaje* policy. This regulation required foreign investors to deposit funds equivalent to 30 per cent of their investment in Chile's central bank. In addition, portfolio investors were required to keep their cash inside the country for a minimum of at least a year. These barriers slowed down the exodus of funds from Chile and kept it from falling victim to what the financial press dubbed Mexico's 'tequila effect'.

Shaken by the Asian debacle, Western finance ministers, led by the US, came up with a new plan to aid countries experiencing balance-of-payments shortfalls before such a crisis occurred. The idea was to give more money (up to $90 billion) and more power to the IMF to create 'an enhanced IMF facility for countries pursuing strong IMF-approved policies'. The thinking was that an instant loan from a 'precautionary fund' would make currency speculators less anxious and so tame the 'hot money' and stall devaluation.

Brazil was the first country to use the new IMF plan. Unfortunately, Brazil's economy seemed no more immune to financial crisis than Indonesia or Thailand. When the Brazilian *real* came under attack in 1998, the government of Fernando Cardoso spent more than $40 billion in foreign exchange trying to prop it up. Cardoso also raised domestic interest rates to 50 per cent to try to keep capital from fleeing the country. Nevertheless traders continued to hammer the *real* even after the country signed a formal letter of intent with the IMF. By January 1999, nearly a billion dollars a day was exiting the country – the government had no choice but to finally devalue its currency, which lost nearly a third of its value overnight.

The Brazilian economy went crashing as IMF policies kicked in. High interest rates scared off domestic business owners who could no longer afford to borrow.

Budget cuts and public-sector layoffs increased poverty and unemployment as the government was forced to implement what the IMF called 'the largest privatization program in history'. As in Asia, the IMF/US Treasury plan championed foreign investment, lured by high interest rates, as Brazil's only long-term hope. Unfortunately, the Fund brushed aside the downside of interest-rate hikes – each percentage increase added millions to debt-service costs, all of which had to be repaid in hard currencies purchased with the devalued Brazilian real. By the end of 1999, Brazil's total external debt, always the highest in the Global South, topped more than $230 billion.

Argentina takes a stand

The next Latin American nation to feel the pinch was Argentina, one of the first Latin nations fervently to embrace globalization. In December 2001, the country sent shockwaves around the world when the economy exploded into social chaos. In less than two weeks, five different presidents tried to take control and calm the increasingly violent demonstrations which had erupted across the country. *'Que se vayan todos!'* the protestors chanted: 'Out with the lot of them!' – meaning all the politicians and the international financiers that had helped bring the country to its knees.

The crisis had its roots in the economic model pushed by the IMF in the early 1990s when Carlos Menem was President. In return for emergency balance-of-payments support, Argentina knocked down its trade barriers, liberalized its capital account and instituted a massive privatization of state enterprises. Nearly 400 companies – from oil and water to steel, insurance, telephone and postal services – were sold off to foreign interests. Corruption was rife: Menem and his cronies grew rich in the process.

But what really attracted speculators was the government's move to peg the Argentine peso to the US dollar at an exchange rate of one-to-one. This effectively removed all control over the domestic economy from the hands of the government. The IMF happily endorsed the arrangement.

Then things began to unravel. With a fixed exchange rate and the dollar rising in value, Argentine goods quickly became uncompetitive, both globally and locally. Cheaper imports flooded the country as the once-thriving agricultural sector slumped. Even the world-famous Argentine beef industry saw export markets dry up. The country had to borrow more foreign currency to finance the growing trade gap, further increasing an already heavy debt burden. Soon lenders began to get the jitters, credit disappeared and businesses lurched into bankruptcy.

In December 2001, Argentina again approached the IMF for a loan to meet its $140-billion external debt. When the Fund balked, the country defaulted on $100 billion of its debt, and then quickly spiraled into recession. In a few short months, unemployment spiked to 21 per cent, GDP declined nearly 17 per cent and more than half of Argentines were living below the poverty line. Something had to give.

Fed up with political corruption and the destructive impact of foreign debt, the Argentine people began to demand more control over their economic lives. The collapse sparked a flurry of worker-run enterprises, co-operatives, alternative currencies, barter exchanges and other self-help institutions. More than 200 companies were taken over and managed by their employees after their owners shut up shop.

In May 2003, the populist government of Nestor Kirchner was elected. In a bold move, Kirchner told debtors he would write off 75 per cent of his country's $100 billion debt in defaulted government bonds – take it or leave it. In September 2003 he also convinced the IMF to roll over $21 billion in outstanding debt, insisting that no more than three per cent of the nation's budget would be used for debt servicing. Pushed to the wall, the IMF caved in.

'We are not going to repeat the history of the past,' said Kirchner. 'For many years we were on our knees before financial organizations and the speculative funds... We've had enough!'[11]

In an astonishing turnaround, the country finally cleared its account with the Fund in January 2006, repaying $9.57 billion in debt and gaining a measure of economic autonomy not felt for decades.

It wasn't easy. Argentina got no help from the IMF along the way. The Fund opposed policies that led to recovery – a stable exchange rate, low interest rates and a tax on exports. A stable currency was important to keep the peso from becoming overvalued. Priced competitively, exports would grow and encourage local investment. Instead the IMF wanted to increase the price of public services like water and electricity, run bigger budget surpluses and pay off foreign creditors. But the Kirchner government held fast – and the economy responded by growing by nearly nine per cent yearly from 2003 to 2006. This was an amazing accomplishment, all the more so because the country continued to service its other debts during that time.

The search for solutions
Despite the obvious danger of capital ricocheting around the globe, the IMF and the US Treasury have been reluctant to support mechanisms to inhibit its movement. And speculators themselves have also been working overtime to squelch defensive government action against their attacks. Pressures to lift exchange controls were strong right up to the most recent 2007/09 financial crisis.

The original Bretton Woods agreement did not fulfill Keynes' dream of giving 'every member government the explicit right to control capital movements', but the policies did give members some controls. Unfortunately, even these limited tools have been gradually eroded over the years by the growing insistence on deregulation. Market fundamentalists like Lawrence Summers, formerly Bill Clinton's Treasury Secretary and now chief economic advisor to Barack Obama, criticized efforts by Malaysia, Hong Kong and others to hobble the movement of overseas capital.

He called controls a 'catastrophe' and urged countries to 'open up to foreign financial service providers, and all the competition, capital and expertise they bring with them'. Given the damage inflicted on millions by the fickle nature of short-term speculators, Summers' views are both short-sighted and harmful. The fact that he is still a powerful Washington insider does not instill confidence that the radical regulatory changes needed to fend off future economic disasters will be made.

As citizens from Korea to Argentina see their lives wrecked by the whipsaw effect of one global financial crisis after another, it is becoming painfully evident that the old ways no longer work. The world has been led to the brink of financial chaos too often over the last few decades. Solutions are needed urgently to ensure that money markets, bond traders and currency speculators are brought under the control of national governments for the public good.

1 See 'Questions and Answers' at www.stampoutpoverty.org. **2** Jagdish Bhagwati, 'The Capital Myth: the difference between the trade in widgets and the trade in dollars', *Foreign Affairs*, May/Jun 1998. **3** Walden Bello, *Dilemmas of Domination*, Zed Books, London, 2005. **4** Walden Bello, 'Domesticating Markets: A social justice perspective on the debate over a new global financial architecture', *Multinational Monitor*, Mar 1999. **5** Testimony of Walden Bello before the House Banking Committee, US House of Representatives, 21 Apr 1998. **6** *Human Development Report 1999*, UNDP/Oxford University Press. **7** Oxfam East Asia Briefing, available from www.oxfam.org.uk **8** Quoted in Mark Weisbrot, 'Globalization for Whom?', Preamble Center, www. preamble. org/globalization **9** Quoted in 'Asian Crisis Spurs Search for New Global Rules', *Economic Justice Report*, Jul 1998. **10** Mark Weisbrot, 'The Case for National Economic Sovereignty', Third World Network Features, Jul 1999. **11** Roger Burbach, 'Can't pay, won't pay', *New Internationalist* No 374, Dec 2004.

6 Poverty, the environment and the market

Faith in economic growth as the key to progress comes into question as the earth's life-support systems fray and signs of ecological collapse multiply. Globalization, geared to spur rapid growth through greater resource consumption, is straining the environment and widening gaps between rich and poor. The standard cure of orthodox market economics – privatization, tax cuts and foreign investment – is not effective. Criticism and concern grows from both expert insiders and grassroots communities.

WHETHER THEY ARE disciples of Keynes, confirmed free-marketers or top-down central planners, economists of all stripes have an abiding faith in the healing powers of economic growth. Keynesians opt for government regulation and an active fiscal policy to kick-start growth in times of economic malaise. They believe the impact of state spending will catalyze the economy, create jobs and stimulate consumption. Keynesians (and the Left in general) have been concerned with making sure that the growing economic pie was distributed fairly. Socialists and some trade unionists have held out for more control over the production process by workers themselves.

Market fundamentalists, sometimes called 'neoliberals', hope to boost consumption using different levers. They opt for 'pure' market solutions – tax cuts and low interest rates – both of which are supposed to increase spending and investment by putting more money into people's pockets.

But, until recently, all sides have ignored the environment. The increasingly global economy is completely dependent on the larger economy of the planet Earth. And evidence is all around us that the planet's ecological health is in trouble.

Poverty, the environment and the market

Our system of industrial production has chewed through massive quantities of non-renewable natural resources over the past two centuries. Not only are we wiping out ecosystems and habitats at an alarming rate, but it is also clear that we are exploiting our natural resource base (the economy's 'natural capital') and generating waste at a rate which exceeds the capacity of the natural world to regenerate and heal itself.

We don't have to look far for proof that growth-centered economics is pushing the regenerative capacities of the planet's ecosystems to the brink. While there is concern that the supply of oil – the most essential non-renewable resource for the industrialized economy – has already peaked, there is no shortage of other raw materials. Even at current rates of consumption there is enough copper, iron and nickel to last centuries. More pressing is the disintegration of the basic life-support systems that we take for granted. The water cycle, the composition of the atmosphere, the assimilation of waste and recycling of nutrients, the pollination of crops, and the delicate interplay of species: all these are in danger.

There is now a large body of research documenting this precipitous decline. Deserts are spreading, forests being hacked down, fertile soils ruined by erosion and desalination, fisheries exhausted, species pushed to extinction, ground water reserves pumped dry. Carbon dioxide levels in the atmosphere continue to rise due to our extravagant burning of fossil fuels. The Intergovernmental Panel on Climate Change, a select group of nearly 2,500 of the world's top climate scientists, says that climate change is unstoppable and will lead to 'widespread economic, social and environmental dislocation over the next century'. Climate change skeptics may scoff but the science is unimpeachable. The UN's Millennium Ecosystem Assessment, released in March 2005, was a stark warning that human activity is putting such strain on the natural functions of the Earth that the ability of the planet's ecosystems to sustain future generations can no longer be taken for granted.

The International Union for Conservation of Nature (IUCN) warns that the global extinction crisis is accelerating, with dramatic declines in populations of many species, including reptiles and primates. The Swiss-based NGO sees habitat loss, human exploitation and invasion by alien species as major threats to wildlife. This loss of habitat is affecting 89 per cent of all threatened birds, 83 per cent of threatened mammals and 91 per cent of threatened plants. The highest number of threatened mammals and birds are found in lowland and mountain tropical rain forests where 900 bird species and 55 per cent of all mammals are threatened.

The IUCN concludes we are losing species faster than any time in history – 1,000 to 10,000 times higher than the natural rate of extinction that occurs through evolution. Between a third and a half of terrestrial species are expected to die out over the next two centuries if current trends continue unchecked. Scientists reckon the normal extinction rate is one species every four years.[1]

Stealing from the future

From 1950 to 2008, global economic output jumped from $4.0 trillion to nearly $60.5 trillion – a 1,500 per cent increase. We have consumed more of the world's natural capital in this brief period than during the entire history of humankind.

The ecologists William Rees and Mathis Wackernagel pioneered the 'ecological footprint' concept, which attempts to put a number on the amount of ecological space occupied by people and by nations. They estimate that around 4-6 hectares of land are used to maintain the consumption of the average person in the West. However, the total available productive land in

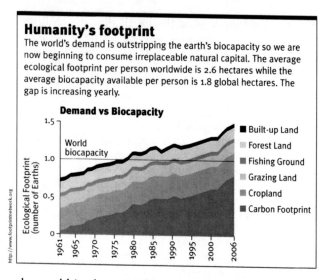

Humanity's footprint

The world's demand is outstripping the earth's biocapacity so we are now beginning to consume irreplaceable natural capital. The average ecological footprint per person worldwide is 2.6 hectares while the average biocapacity available per person is 1.8 global hectares. The gap is increasing yearly.

the world is about 1.7 hectares per person (total land divided by population). The difference they call 'appropriated carrying capacity' – which basically means the rich are living off the resources of the poor.

The Netherlands, for example, consumes the output of a productive land mass 14 times its size. Most Northern countries and many urban regions in the South already consume more than their fair share; they depend on trade (using someone else's natural assets) or on depleting their own natural capital. According to Rees and Wackernagel, the global footprint now exceeds global biocapacity by 20 per cent and that gap is growing yearly. The US alone, with 4.5 per cent of the world's population, sucks up 25 per cent of the earth's biocapacity. The average Indian has a global footprint of just 0.8 hectares while the average American has an ecological footprint of 9.7 hectares.[2]

Regions like North America and western Europe, argue Rees and Wackernagel, 'run an unaccounted ecological deficit – their population either appropriating carrying capacity from elsewhere or from future generations'.[3]

Faith in economic growth as the ultimate hope for human progress is widespread. A central tenet of economists on both Left and Right has been that the 'carrying capacity' of the Earth is infinitely expandable. The underlying belief is that a combination of ingenuity and technology will eventually allow us all to live like middle-class Americans – if only we can ignore the naysayers and keep the economy growing.

Unfortunately, this doesn't look likely. As the Worldwatch Institute points out: 'Rising demand for energy, food and raw materials by 2.5 billion Chinese and Indians is already having ripple effects worldwide... If China and India were to consume resources and produce pollution at the current US per capita level, it would require two planet Earths just to sustain their two economies.'[2]

Says ecologist Robert Ayres: 'There is every indication that human economic activity, supported by perverse trade and growth policies, is well on the way to perturbing our natural environment more and faster than any known event in planetary history.'[4]

Ayres is on to something when he accuses the 'perverse' aspects of globalization of accelerating the process of environmental decline. Export-led growth and Third World debt have combined to speed up the rapid consumption of the Earth's irreplaceable natural resources. Some environmentalists argue that primary resources (nature's goods and services) are too cheap and that their market price does not reflect either their finite nature or the hidden social and ecological costs of extraction. Instead, they suggest, we should conserve the resources we have by making them more expensive. There is some truth to this analysis. The price of raw materials is notoriously unpredictable, based not just on supply and demand but also on the monopoly power of corporations that control distribution and sales.

Poverty, the environment and the market

In general, when the global economy booms, overall demand goes up; when the economy crashes, as it did in 2007-08, demand falls. In recent years, the price of industrial metals like nickel, copper and iron has risen (or fallen) in tandem with the Chinese economy. On the other hand, world market prices for commodities like cotton, sugar and coffee have never been lower. In 2007, just before the global meltdown, when the world price of energy nearly tripled, all commodity prices rose sharply, including the price of staples like corn and rice.

But debt in the developing countries, the source of many of the world's commodities, has also kept prices low. Centuries of colonialism put in place a system of extreme dependency on a narrow range of primary exports which remains to this day. According to UNCTAD, just three commodities account for 75 per cent of total exports in each of the 48 poorest nations. This might be tolerable if nations like Honduras, Kenya and Zambia earned a decent income from their sugar, tea and copper. Sadly, the opposite is true. Due to plunging 'terms of trade', commodity-dependent nations need to export more and more every year just to stay in the same place. From 1997 to 2001, the combined price index of all commodities fell by 53 per cent – raw exports lost half their purchasing power in terms of manufactured goods. According to UNCTAD, exporters of primary agricultural products saw their terms of trade continue to decline from 2004 to 2006.

'Adjustment' policies imposed by the IMF/World Bank as the price of admission to the global trading community mean that poor countries are obliged to service their debts before they are allowed to do anything else. They have little choice but to try and expand commodity exports to world markets. Unfortunately, removing the barriers to exports isn't always the answer. In fact, it can make matters worse, especially in the agricultural sector. When farmers grow more for export, it often leads, perversely, to overproduction and lower prices. Faced with lower earnings, farmers respond rationally by increasing their production even more. Added to this desperate cycle is the black hole of debt: countries in hock have been forced by World Bank and IMF structural adjustment edicts to ratchet up exports to service their debts. The new term circulating among critical economists to describe the phenomenon is 'immiserating trade'. The more you trade, the poorer you get.[5]

And therein lies the problem. Because all poor countries have to increase their exports at once, there is a glut and prices fall – sometimes by half. Twice as much has to be exported to earn the same amount of foreign currency. The beneficiaries are the developed countries and Western-based corporations. They not only get their debts serviced, but they also benefit from cheap commodities that keep prices down, profits up and inflation under control in the North. The losers are the people of the South – those who depend on non-petroleum primary exports – and the global environment.

Deregulated destruction
Globalization policies put the squeeze on the environment in other ways, too. Take the case of Brazil, which environmentalists consider one of the earth's most ecologically important nations. The country still contains 30 per cent of the planet's rainforest, long considered to be 'the lungs of the world'. Scientists believe the spectacular biological diversity of the rainforest is a potential cornucopia of priceless, life-saving drugs.

In 1999 the Brazilian government slashed millions of dollars off environmental spending in the wake of IMF-enforced cuts. The country's environmental enforcement arm had its budget reduced by 19 per cent. In addition, the domestic recession brought on by IMF policies boosted unemployment, forcing many ordinary workers and peasants to clear larger areas of jungle for subsistence.

Encouraging primary exports can also strengthen the hand of agribusiness and large landowners. Peasant farmers and smallholders are squeezed out by the implacable logic of economic efficiency. In Brazil, the amount of land devoted to large-scale soy production has jumped from 200,000 hectares to 12 million hectares over the past 30 years, much of it virgin rainforest. The growth of the country's beef industry has caused even more environmental destruction in the Amazon. In 2004, 27,000 square kilometers of rainforest was burned, the second highest rate on record, mostly due to cattle ranching. Over the past 40 years, about a fifth of Brazil's Amazon rainforest has been deforested, an average of 20,000 square kilometers per year over the last 10 years. Brazil is now the world's biggest beef exporter but the industry's continued expansion threatens 40 per cent of the world's remaining rainforest.[6]

Dr Gustavo Fonseca of the *Universidade Federal de Minas Gerais* in Brazil sums up the concern of environmentalists: 'Our biggest worry now is that the government is going to lose control of attempts to control deforestation. This is undermining the very basis of what we've been trying to accomplish in Brazil.'[7]

Even before the crash of 1997, part of Asia's 'economic miracle' had been built on a fast-track liquidation of its natural resources. Pristine rainforests were plundered, rivers despoiled, sea coasts poisoned with pesticides and fisheries exhausted. In the Indonesian capital, Jakarta, more than 70 per cent of water samples were found to be 'highly contaminated by chemical pollutants' while the country's forests were being hacked down at the rate of 2.4

million hectares per year. In the Malaysian state of Sarawak (part of the island of Borneo) 30 per cent of the forest disappeared in a mere two decades, while in peninsular Malaysia 73 per cent of 116 rivers surveyed by authorities were found to be either 'biologically dead' or 'dying'.[8]

The environmental group Friends of the Earth (FoE) summarized the impact of free-market deregulation on Third World environments in its 1999 study, *IMF: selling the environment short.* FoE examined IMF policies in eight countries, including Cameroon, Côte d'Ivoire, Guyana, Nicaragua and Thailand, and found significant negative environmental impacts in all of them.

Several countries slashed government spending after being pressured by the Fund to eliminate budget deficits. The report also noted that IMF policies encourage, and sometimes induce, countries to exploit natural resources at unsustainable rates. According to Carol Welch, co-author of the report: 'Every case shows that the IMF pushes short-term profit at the expense of biodiversity and ecological prosperity... the IMF is undermining people's lives by disregarding environmental issues.'[9]

Persistent poverty has also spurred environmental decline – the desperately poor do not make good ecocitizens. Tribal peoples plunder the forest on which they depend for survival; animals are poached and slaughtered by impoverished African villagers for their valuable ivory, their body parts or simply for 'bush meat'.

Madagascar, an island once covered in lush forests, has turned into a barren wasteland as local people slash and burn jungle plots to grow food. The huge Indian Ocean island is home to some 200,000 plant and animal species – three-quarters of which are found nowhere else. Less than a tenth of Madagascar is still tree-covered and the forest is vanishing at the rate of 200,000 hectares a year. Poverty is the core of the problem: 70 per cent of the island's 14 million people live on less than a dollar a day.

'Our village has been burning forests to plant rice here for generations,' Dimanche Dimasy, chief elder of Mahatsara village, told the BBC. 'This is our way of life. If we can't cut the forests, we can't feed ourselves. The government wants to protect the forests but nobody cares about protecting the peasants who live here.'[10]

Cracks in the consensus

The logic of globalization is seductive because it is based on a simple principle: free the market of constraints and its self-evolving dynamic will bring employment, wealth and prosperity. But, despite the confidence of those who preach the gospel of free markets, there are clear indications that some people are losing their faith.

The signs are inescapable – not least of which are the thousands of civil-society groups around the world who have begun to take their protests to the streets. It began in Seattle in November 1999 when more than 50,000 people from dozens of countries demonstrated at the annual meeting of the World Trade Organization. The gathering was a unique mix of environmentalists, trade unionists, peasant groups, students and ordinary citizens – all united by their concern that economic globalization is spinning out of control. The protest gained worldwide prominence when police in riot gear charged the crowds, firing pepper gas, teargas and plastic bullets. Some 500 people were arrested and a state of emergency declared.

Then, at the spring meetings of the IMF and World Bank in April 2000, another 15,000 people gathered in Washington for a repeat protest. Ironically, the same week, as if to underline the demonstrators' critique of globalization, stock markets nosedived as a wave of panic selling swept the globe, puncturing the high-tech stock bubble that had carried markets to dizzying new heights through the 1990s. After Seattle, civil-society demonstrations became a regular occurrence at meetings of the Bretton Woods trio or the G8 – Prague in October 2000, Quebec City in April 2001, Genoa in July 2001, Miami in November 2003, Gleneagles, Scotland, in July 2005 and L'Aquila, Italy, in July 2009. Everywhere the proponents of economic globalization now meet they run into a similar phalanx of protesters.

Even among mainstream economists globalization is coming under increasing scrutiny. The financial crises in Russia, Asia and Latin America in the late 1990s proved to be a warm-up for the spectacular global crash of 2007/09. Together they have opened deep rifts in the dominant 'Washington Consensus' – a view which had been advocated by the Bretton Woods institutions and endorsed by most Western governments. Powerful voices that had previously backed free trade and market liberalization began to speak out.

The influential economist Jeffrey Sachs was one of those. Now Director of The Earth Institute at Columbia University and Special Advisor to UN Secretary-General Ban Ki-moon, Sachs was an IMF advisor and one of the main engineers of capitalist 'shock therapy' in Russia after the fall of the Soviet Union. The Asian débâcle forced him to re-examine his faith in the supremacy of free markets and to question some of the conventional solutions to national financial crises – especially the role of the IMF. In a candid *Financial Times* article published in December 1997, Sachs called the IMF 'secretive' and 'unaccountable'. 'It defies logic,' he said, that 'a small group of 1,000 economists on 19th Street in Washington should dictate the economic conditions of life to 75 developing countries with around 1.4 billion people.'

Poverty, the environment and the market

Others began to speak out too. The World Bank's former Chief Economist, Joseph Stiglitz, became a much-quoted 'ex-insider' willing to criticize publicly the conservative policies of market fundamentalists.

Globalization and its Discontents, his scathing 2002 critique of the Bretton Woods institutions, became a bestseller, studded with personal anecdotes and case studies.

'The net effect of the policies set by the Washington consensus,' he wrote, 'has all too often been to benefit the few at the expense of the many, the well-off at the expense of the poor. In many cases commercial interests and values have superseded concern for the environment, democracy, human rights, and social justice.'[11]

Stiglitz continues to hammer away at the dangers of unregulated markets. During the economic crash of 2007-09 he told Britain's *Guardian* newspaper: 'There was a moment of euphoria when we were all Keynesians. It was not just Keynesian macro-economic policies, it was the need for regulation and the recognition that economics had failed.' Now, he says, the forces of the status quo have regrouped. 'The optimist in me is hopeful that we won't need another crisis to finally motivate the political process. The pessimist in me says that it may need to happen.'[12]

Despite the spectacular economic growth of the past half-century, the quality of life for a fifth of the world's population has actually regressed in relative, and sometimes absolute, terms. One of the most cogent critiques of the downside of globalization comes from the UN Development Programme. Its yearly *Human Development Report* is a first-rate compilation of insightful data and cogent, probing analysis. It's not journalism but it gets to the point. 'When the market goes too far in dominating social and political outcomes, the opportunities and rewards of globalization spread unequally and inequitably – concentrating power and wealth in a select group of people, nations and corporations, marginalizing the others.'[13]

The UN agency supports its analysis with hard-hitting figures on what it calls a 'grotesque and dangerous polarization' between those people and countries benefiting from the system and those that are merely 'passive recipients' of its effects.

Even on its own terms, economic globalization is not working for the majority of the world's citizens. As Joseph Stiglitz points outs: 'Despite repeated promises of poverty reduction made over the last decade of the 20th century, the actual number of people living in poverty has actually increased by 100 million.'[11]

Mind the gap

Despite an apparent increase in global growth and steadily increasing per capita income, the gap both within and between rich and poor countries is widening.

- The richest fifth of the world's population receives more than 75% of world income while the poorest 20% receives just 1.5%.
- 2.5 billion people living on less than $2 a day – 40% of the world's population – receive only 5% of global income.
- Of the 73 countries for which figures are available, 53 (with over 80% of the world's population) have seen income inequality increase from 1990-2005.
- During the same period, the income gap between the top and bottom 10 per cent of wage earners increased in 70 per cent of those same countries.

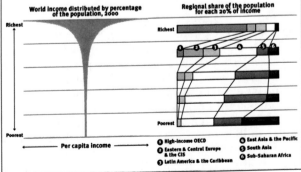

World income distributed by percentage of the population, 2000

Regional share of the population for each 20% of income

Richest

Poorest

Per capita income

❶ High-income OECD
❷ Eastern & Central Europe & the CIS
❸ Latin America & the Caribbean
❹ East Asia & the Pacific
❺ South Asia
❻ Sub-Saharan Africa

Human Development Report 2005, UN Development Programme, New York 2005 and World of Work Report 2008, ILO, Geneva, 2008.

Poverty, the environment and the market

In 1960, the fifth of the world's people who live in the richest countries had 30 times more income than the fifth living in the poorest countries. By 1997 the income gap had more than doubled. According to UNDP, the top five per cent of the world's population had an income 114 times greater than the bottom five per cent; while the world's richest 500 individuals have a combined income greater than that of the poorest 416 million.

Income inequality is increasing in countries that account for more than 80 per cent of the world's population. And the growing gap can mean life or death: children born into the poorest 20 per cent of households in Ghana or Senegal are two to three times more likely to die before the age of five than children born into the richest 20 per cent of households.[14]

The widening gap

Another UN study, this one on income inequality in OECD countries, concluded that in the 1980s real wages (adjusted for inflation) had fallen and income inequality increased in all countries except Germany and Italy.

In the US, the top 10 per cent of families boosted their average income by 16 per cent while the top 1 per cent increased theirs by a whopping 50 per cent. This trend was echoed elsewhere. In Latin America the top 10 per cent of wage-earners increased their share while the poorest 10 per cent saw their income drop by 15 per cent, wiping out what meager improvements they had made in the previous decade. Income inequality also grew in Thailand, Indonesia, China and other Asian nations, even though the region enjoyed healthy economic growth throughout the decade. China, for example, had 250,000 US dollar millionaires in 2005, less than 0.4 per cent of the population, who held 70 per cent of the country's wealth.[15] In Sub-Saharan Africa, the situation is worse: after two decades of IMF/World Bank structural adjustment income inequality is not only growing but per capita incomes are falling. They are now lower than they were in 1990. The region has 100 million more people living on less than a dollar a day than it did a decade earlier.

This shift in wealth and income from bottom to top is part of the logic of globalization. In order to be 'competitive', governments adopt policies which cut taxes and favor profits over wages. The economic argument is simple: putting more money into the pockets of corporations and wealthy individuals (who benefit most from tax cuts: the higher the income the greater the gain) is supposed to lead to greater investment, jobs, economic growth and prosperity. Corporate tax rates have dropped across the industrialized world over the past decade. In the US in 2007, the richest 400 taxpayers increased their incomes by 31 per cent over the previous year and paid an even lower effective tax rate. The average income of the richest 400 grew from $263.3 million in 2006 to $344.8 million in 2007 while their effective income tax rate fell from 17.17 per cent to 16.62 per cent. Effective corporate tax rates in the US dropped from 27 per cent to 17 per cent in the 1988-2003 period.[16]

Unfortunately, there is no evidence that improvements in public well-being result from tax cuts for the rich or lower wages for the rest of us. If the reverse were true and tax cuts were directed towards those at the bottom of the income ladder there might be some impact. The money would almost certainly be spent on basic necessities rather than luxury goods. But this isn't part of the globalization game plan. In every country that has taken up the 'reduce-taxes-cut-the-deficit' mantra the majority of tax cuts benefit wealthy individuals and corporations. What happens to the money is perhaps predictable: some goes into high-priced consumer baubles – a phenomenon which is glaringly visible amongst the élite in cities from Bangkok to Los Angeles. But most winds up in the stock market or in other sorts of non-productive speculation.

Major players are no longer satisfied with modest profits on long-term investment, especially when double-digit returns are available by gambling in currency speculation or derivatives. This diversion of capital away from socially useful investment is one of the major forces fueling the 'casino economy'. That and the fact that investment opportunities in the goods-producing sector are shrinking due to the problem of 'over-capacity' – too many goods chasing too few buyers (see chapter 5). Computerized robots and automated assembly lines replace workers with new technology, leaving fewer people actually to buy the products that factories are churning out. Those that remain find their wages under constant downward pressure in the face of cheaper labor elsewhere. The drive to be competitive ends up being a 'race to the bottom'. Workers who don't lose their jobs find their wages squeezed.

In Canada, which normally ranks near the top of UNDP's annual 'human development' table, a recent study found that real disposable income on average fell by 3.3 per cent between 1989 and 1999. This coincided exactly with a period of neoliberal economic policies, including drastic cuts in government expenditures, reduced taxes and relatively high domestic interest rates. In 2008, Canada's top 100 corporate bosses earned 174 times more than the average Canadian worker, according to the Canadian Center for Policy Alternatives.

Despite these worrying warning signs, staunch free marketers are reluctant to abandon their beliefs: 'Give the private sector the resources,' they say, 'it will do the job.' But the proof is elusive. Surplus capital which doesn't get funneled into currency markets zips straight into overseas tax havens where both rich individuals and globe-trotting transnationals have been squirreling away their cash for decades.

There are nearly 70 tax havens scattered around the world. These 'offshore financial centers' include places like the Bahamas, the Cayman Islands, Monaco, Luxembourg and Bermuda. Investors can store their wealth secretly, no questions asked – thus escaping any social obligations to the country where they may have earned it. Only a small number of these tax havens have public disclosure laws affecting the banks which operate within their borders.

The Economist estimates that the 1.2 per cent of the world population who live in tax havens produce about 3 per cent of the global GDP. Yet these countries account for 26 per cent of the world's financial assets and more than 30 per cent of the profits of US transnationals. This final figure gives a clear sense of how important tax havens are to the corporate world – and why they need to be closed. But it also underlines the flawed reasoning of those who support economic policies premised on tax cuts and corporate deregulation. In almost all cases, corporations will do whatever they can to avoid paying taxes. Private companies exist to maximize returns on the investment of their stockholders – they jeopardize their own survival to the extent that they are unable to reach that goal.

Enron example

This tension between the corporate world view and the broader public interest is one reason why tax havens are now coming under intense scrutiny. Countries in the Organization of Economic Cooperation and Development (OECD) and in the EU have long recognized these havens as a drain on national treasuries and a convenient way of 'laundering' illegal funds. For example, the disgraced US energy trading company, Enron, is said to have used 800 different 'financial dumps' in the Caribbean to hide its debts.

And it is estimated that up to $500 billion from the global narcotics trade passes through tax havens annually. There is now fear that the rise of electronic commerce, combined with global financial liberalization, will trigger an even greater flow of wealth and profits to these tax-free enclaves.[17]

While the numbers of the super-wealthy expand, the social fabric that forms the backdrop to all our lives continues to fray. This is the hidden human cost of 'market discipline' and it is as much a dilemma for European social democracies as it is for countries in Africa or Latin America.

All of us in the industrialized nations can chronicle the gradual decline in public services and social provision that has accompanied attempts to control government deficits. This cut-back on public spending is demanded by international markets – by the same investors that demand higher rates of return on their investment and lower rates of taxation. As corporate profits boom and real wages stagnate, the glue that holds us together is losing its bond. Government revenues are steered to paying down debt or cutting taxes while citizens are told there is no longer enough money to pay for 'public goods'. Middle-class taxpayers, offered a few hundred dollars in cuts, in return receive deteriorating schools, reduced funding for parks and recreation facilities, inadequate public transport and a weakened healthcare system.

In western Europe, Canada, Australia and New Zealand/Aotearoa, public education and healthcare systems have seen repeated budget cuts as the state retreats and makes way for private, profit-oriented ventures. Welfare and unemployment benefits have been 'rationalized', slashing the number of those eligible. Senior citizens and those nearing retirement are fearful that promised pensions will evaporate as governments become more desperate for funds.

Individuals are frantically scraping together whatever savings they have and heading towards the stock market in the hope that they too will ride to old-age security on the coattails of the FTSE, the NASDAQ and the Dow Jones. Tapping into the politics of resentment, some governments are attempting to claw back the hard-won gains of public sector workers in an attempt to bring everyone down to the same low level of pensions or benefits. Government funding for the arts and for environmental protection has also been steadily eroded. The failure to protect these 'public goods' diminishes us all, makes us less capable of caring for each other and prohibits us from advancing together as a cohesive, mutually supportive community.

Globalization has also derailed development in the South, where the poor continue to pay the highest price of adjustment. In order to boost exports and maintain their obligations to creditors, developing countries must divert money away from things like healthcare, education and aid to small-scale farmers. There have been countless studies detailing the social impact of economic globalization and the results are depressingly similar. The poor feel the biggest impact. In most of the world's poorest countries, poverty reduction stalled between 1995 and 2005 as they fell further behind richer nations. The most recent global recession will only worsen this trend.

As Brazil's economy lurched into crisis in 1998, the IMF insisted on huge government cuts approaching a fifth of the budget. More than eight million of Brazil's poorest depend on subsidized rations of beans, rice and sugar for survival. The Government was forced to cut expenditure on those rations by more than half. At the same time the subsidy on school lunches was cut by 35 per cent. The 1999 budget for land reform, one of the most pressing social issues in Latin America, was reduced by 43 per cent.

Poverty, the environment and the market

Indian liberalization

The Indian government launched its campaign to liberalize the economy and open up to foreign investors in 1992. Almost two decades later the giant nation has been transformed. Transnational brands are ubiquitous and sleek Japanese cars now jostle bullock carts in the streets of Mumbai and Hyderabad. High-tech exports are booming. In January 2006, Dell Inc, the world's biggest personal computer maker, announced that it would open a fourth call center in the country, increasing its Indian workforce to 15,000. Meanwhile, the country is graduating millions of skilled professionals and foreign capital is pouring in. Microsoft, Intel and Cisco all announced investments of a billion dollars or more in early 2006.[18] Investment in the IT industry in India was worth an estimated $71.6 billion in 2009, according to the accounting firm KPMG.

Nonetheless, opposition has been growing as disparities within the country widen. A 1997 Gallup poll found that two out of three Indians believed their standard of living had fallen or stagnated since embracing globalization. India has the largest number of poor people in a single country. An estimated 350-400 million of its nearly 1 billion citizens live below the poverty line, 75 per cent of them in the rural areas. Malnutrition affects half the country's children and 10 per cent of all boys and a quarter of all girls don't attend primary school, while the death rate for girls age 1-5 is 50 per cent greater than for boys.[13] Demonstrations have erupted across the country as Indians worry about cheap food imports wiping out local farmers. Two influential coalitions uniting hundreds of grassroots organizations are spearheading the protests. The National Alliance of Peoples' Movements is made up of more than 200 citizens' groups and was formed in 1993. The Joint Forum of Indian People Against Globalization (JAFIP) brought together more than 50 farmers' and peasant groups in

1998 to demand that India withdraw from the WTO.

The litany of suffering and damage spawned by harsh market reforms is repeated across the developing world.

A massive study involving hundreds of civil-society groups across eight countries confirms this judgment. The Structural Adjustment Participatory Review Initiative (SAPRI) held hearings from Bangladesh to El Salvador gathering grassroots information over a four-year period, originally with the participation of ex-World Bank President Jim Wolfensohn. However, the Bank backed out of the process when it realized what would appear in the final report. No wonder. The SAPRI review confirmed what Northern NGOs and ordinary people in the South had been saying for years: 'Adjustment policies contributed to further impoverishment and marginalization of local populations while increasing economic inequality.'[19]

In Senegal, which had endured 20 years of IMF programs, the report found 'declining quality in education and health' combined with a growth in 'maternal mortality, unemployment and child labor'. In Tanzania, globalization had successfully redirected agriculture towards exports but had also 'expanded rural poverty, income inequality and environmental degradation'. Food security decreased, housing conditions deteriorated and primary-school enrollment dropped, while malnutrition and infant mortality rose.

In Mexico, millions of farmers were pushed out of agriculture and thousands of small businesses went bankrupt. A decade after NAFTA, poverty, rural unemployment and overall inequality had all increased. In 1990, Mexico was self-sufficient in maize. Today it's the world's third-largest importer. According to an Oxfam report, after free trade poor Mexicans became dependent on 'bought seeds, on controlled and unequal markets and on powerful middlemen'.[20]

Poverty, the environment and the market

In Nicaragua, whose mildly leftist Sandinista government was destabilized by the US in the 1980s, IMF policies drove the country into further poverty. Financial deregulation attracted capital to 'short-term, high-interest deposits' and 'away from productive investment in small-scale domestic agriculture and manufacturing'. In Hungary, the IMF advised introducing liberalized trade, a tight money supply and rapid privatization of state assets. But the report found the policies deflected money away from education and social services and into the wallets of wealthy bond holders.

Poverty in Russia

But it was Russia, after the break-up of the Soviet Union, where the orthodox prescription for economic reform did some of its greatest harm. Supported by billions in Western aid, subsidized loans and rescheduled debt, the plan was to turn Russia into a capitalist success story. Instead the 'shock therapy' threw the economy open to the winds of corruption. State assets were privatized, ending up in the hands of a small group of powerful insiders (often the same people who ran the former communist state apparatus) while ordinary Russians were saddled with colossal debts. At the same time an estimated $150 billion left the country, most of it permanently.

In the absence of price controls, and with the loss of guaranteed employment, Russians endured poverty unknown for decades. From 1998 to 2000, more than 40 million Russians were forced below the poverty line. Today, 25 per cent live below the poverty line and incomes are lower than they were in 1990. The country experienced the steepest fall in peacetime living standards in modern history. According to the UN, inequality doubled from 1989 to 1996. The income share of the richest 20 per cent of Russians was 11 times that of the poorest 20 per cent. Male life expectancy dropped from 70 years in the mid-1980s to 59 years in 2005. By 1996 the under-five child mortality rate was 25 per thousand live births – the same as Libya or Venezuela.[21]

In all countries touched by economic globalization, women tend to bear a disproportionate share of the costs. One feminist critique of structural adjustment documented many ways in which women become 'shock absorbers' for economic reforms. These include: forcing more women into 'informal' sector jobs as mainstream opportunities fade; promoting export crops which men tend to dominate; disrupting girls' education; increasing mortality rates and worsening female health; more domestic violence and stress; and an overall increase in the workload of women both inside and outside the home.[22]

Since women are the caregivers in most societies, they tend to pick up the pieces when the social safety net is slashed. A 1997 Zimbabwe study found that 15 years of economic reform had a devastating impact on women in that southern African country. When school fees were raised, girls dropped out first. And when health spending was cut by a third, the number of women dying in childbirth doubled. As male bread-winners are laid off, women do what they can to compensate for the lost income. They brew beer, turn to prostitution or become street traders. It inevitably falls on women to pick up the slack when governments cut education, healthcare and other social programs.[9]

Are the social and environmental costs of economic growth too great? As the victims of globalization multiply, growing legions of ordinary people are beginning to question a process over which they have no control and little say. It's easy to be a cheerleader for globalization if you're on the winning side. But not so easy if your job has been outsourced to Mexico or China, or your coffee crop no longer brings in enough cash to feed and clothe your family. As the sinews of the global economy bind tighter, millions of ordinary people around the world have begun to speak out forcefully against a system which they see as both harmful and unjust.

Instead of a homogenized global culture shaped by the narrow demands of the 'money economy', there is a resurgent push for equity and sustainability. Instead of a deregulated globalization which rides roughshod over the rights of nation-states and communities, civil-society groups from Bolivia to China are calling for a radical restructuring. The aim is for an economic system more connected to real human needs and aspirations – and less geared to the anti-human machinations of the corporate-led free market. In the next chapter we'll look at how we might get there.

1 www.millenniumassessment.org/en/index.aspx. 2 C Flavin and G Gardner, 'China, India and the New World Order', State of the World 2006, WW Norton, New York, 2006. 3 Mathis Wackernagel and William Rees, Our Ecological Footprint: reducing human impact on human health, New Society Publishers, 1996. 4 Quoted in Kalle Lasn, 'The global economy is a doomsday machine', see www.adbusters.org/campaigns/economic-globaldoomsday.html 5 Gerald Greenfield, 'Free market freefall', Focus on the Global South, www.focusweb.org 6 George Monbiot, 'The price of cheap beef', The Guardian, 18 Oct 2005. 7 Anthony Faiola, 'Brazil's sick economy infects the ecosystem', Guardian Weekly, 25 Apr 1999. 8 Walden Bello, 'The end of the miracle', Multinational Monitor, Jan/Feb 1998. 9 Friends of the Earth, The IMF: selling the environment short, see www.foe.org/res/pubs/pdf/imf.pdf 10 Tim Cocks, 'Malagasy Wilderness in the Balance', BBC News, 14 Feb 2005, http://news.bbc.co.uk/2/ hi/africa/4258781.stm 11 Joseph Stiglitz, Globalization and its Discontents, WW Norton, New York, 2002. 12 Larry Elliott, 'Lesson of credit crunch hasn't been learned', The Guardian, 12 Feb 2010. 13 Human Development Report 1999 (UNDP, New York, 1999). 14 Human Development Report 2005 (UNDP, New York, 2005). 15 Martin Hart-Landsberg, 'The US economy and China', Monthly Review, Feb 2010. 16 'Bush Policies Drive Surge in Corporate Tax Freeloading', see www.ctj.org/corpfedo4pr.pdf 17 Madelaine Drohan, 'No mean feat to crack down on tax havens', The Globe and Mail, Toronto, 12 Apr 2000. 18 'Dell to add 5,000 employees in India', Toronto Star, 31 Jan 2006. 19 'The policy roots of economic crisis and poverty', www.saprin.org/global_rpt.htm 20 Oxfam Connections, 'Fair Trade vs Free Trade', Sep 2002, www.oxfam.org.au/publications/connections/september_2002/fairtradevsfreetrade.html 21 'Robbing Russia', The Nation, 4 Oct 1999. 22 P Sparr, Mortgaging women's lives, Zed Press, 1994.

7 Redesigning the global economy

Globalization is increasing inequality and poverty worldwide as national governments lose the ability to control their development strategies and policies. Political solutions are needed to reinvigorate democratic control both North and South. But political reforms need to be combined with structural reforms. These should put meaningful employment and human rights at the heart of economic policy, boost local control and decision-making and restore the ecological health and natural capital of our planet.

ECONOMIC GLOBALIZATION IS a powerful movement of people, goods, capital and ideas – driven by ideology, self-interest and bottom-line notions of economic efficiency.

But it is, essentially, an undemocratic process – one that is proceeding without the approval or knowledge of hundreds of millions of people who are most directly affected by the great economic upheavals of the last quarter century.

While it is true that globalization has accelerated growth and lifted millions out of poverty, the process has been, at best, uneven. And it has left inequality and environmental devastation in its wake. It has also been highly selective. Most of the gains have been in Asia, especially in China and India. New investment in those countries has reduced the numbers of extreme poor by half a billion people since 1990.

China has morphed into the new Manchester, flooding the world with mass-produced consumer goods. The Chinese economy has been on a tear. As the rest of the world slumped, China's economy grew by 8.7 per cent in 2009. The country uses more than a quarter of the world's steel and nearly half its cement. It's also the world's second-largest oil consumer after the US, and the world's biggest producer and consumer of coal.

Redesigning the global economy

The Chinese auto industry is beginning to spread its wings and Western car manufacturers are cowering. The Chinese firms Geely, Chery and Lifan Group are poised to fill world markets with cheap, fuel-efficient cars. In less than two decades its economy will outstrip the United States. The investment bank, Goldman Sachs, predicts it will be number one by 2026. The country's total share of world exports rose from 1.8 per cent to 9.1 per cent from 1990 to 2008.[1]

Unfortunately, growth in both China and India has come at a huge cost: poisoned water, deadly air, depleted soils, the world's worst acid rain, and the largest migration from the countryside to the urban areas in history.

According to the Worldwatch Institute: 'Land degradation, depleted aquifers, water pollution and urban claims on land and water are nibbling away at China and India's agricultural foundations – and may soon make it impossible for them to meet their rapidly expanding food needs.'[2]

Rapid growth has also heightened regional disparities and increased the gap between rich and poor. On average, workers in Indian cities earn nearly 40 per cent more than those in the countryside. In China, wage gaps are greatest between the booming eastern cities and the poorer rural areas. According to an Asian Development Bank study of 22 countries, China is now East Asia's second most unequal country after Nepal. Annual incomes in Beijing and Shanghai average more than $1,000 while rural incomes are closer to $370. China still has 600 million citizens living on less than $2 a day and India has another 800 million in the same boat. Fearing social unrest as inequality grows, President Hu Jintao has admitted that China needs to build a 'more balanced and harmonious society'.

Meanwhile, globalization has completely ignored other parts of the world. In sub-Saharan Africa, between 1990 and 2002, per-capita income didn't rise at all. The number of people living on less than a dollar a day increased by a third, to more than 330 million. As UNDP notes, income inequality is increasing in countries that account for more than 80 per cent of the world's population.

The conclusion seems unavoidable: economic globalization has tragically failed the world's poor. Says Indian economist Jayati Ghosh: 'Despite popular perceptions, a net transfer of jobs from North to South did not take place. In fact, industrial employment in the South barely increased in the past decade, even in China. Instead, technological change meant fewer workers could generate more output. Old jobs in the South were lost or became precarious and the majority of new jobs were insecure and low paying.'[3]

As it is impoverishing millions, North and South, it is also radically altering social relationships, stripping age-old cultures of their identity and threatening the environmental health of the Earth.

There is no doubt that the promise of globalization – greater wealth and material prosperity for all – is compelling and that the forces behind it are formidable. But a top-down, unequal globalization is not inevitable. We have the power to make the system work in a more just way. The economic structures that shape production and distribution are human-made. The institutions that make the rules governing the operation of the world economy are human-made. And the politicians that we elect to govern us are people too. Change is possible.

The crisis of globalization is a unique opportunity to address core issues of democracy and human development. It has invigorated a worldwide people's movement whose loud demands for change are attracting more and more attention and support: from consumers, environmentalists, trade unionists, women's groups, religious activists, farmers, human rights advocates and ordinary citizens.

Redesigning the global economy

Social Forum movement

The World Social Forum is one of the most visible expressions of opposition – an annual gathering of thousands of such groups from around the globe. The WSF was born in the aftermath of massive demonstrations against the World Trade Organization in Seattle in November 1999. It was initially organized to coincide with the annual gathering of political and business leaders at the World Economic Forum in Davos, Switzerland. The first three WSF meetings were held in Porto Alegre, Brazil. The fourth forum in Mumbai in 2004 drew more than 100,000 people. The 2006 forum was held in three different centers to encourage more regional collaboration – Caracas, Karachi and Bamako, Mali while the 2011 meeting will be held in Dakar, Senegal. Activists from more than 150 countries have attended these huge events but the WSF has also spawned dozens of local, regional and national social forums. These face-to-face encounters provide citizens' groups with a chance to compare notes, to strategize and to hammer out alternatives to the prevailing model of economic globalization. This is not an anti-globalization movement as much as it is a pro-peoples movement. The motto of the WSF is 'another world is possible'. It is, in essence, a network of networks focusing on global issues of social and economic justice, interacting when necessary, but mostly working independently on their own issues in their own countries or communities.

The Social Forum movement has so far managed to avoid fracturing into sectarianism and has avoided alliance with specific political parties – to its credit. As the saying goes, 'politics is the art of compromise'. The WSF understands that, in order to influence change, the movement needs to remain independent of formal politics, acting both as a conscience and a goad. And there is good reason for this. The powerful gatekeepers of the global economic system can force even the most socially progressive political leaders into tight corners. Yesterday's hero, bravely confronting the IMF or the WTO, can quickly become tomorrow's victim of the 'Washington Consensus'.

Other campaigns to rein in the globalization juggernaut have succeeded in educating millions about global inequalities. The Jubilee 2000 campaign to cancel Third World debt galvanized thousands of supporters, both North and South. More recently, the Make Poverty History movement and the global Trade Justice Campaign have continued to push for significant changes to the world trading system to improve the lives of the world's poor.

Speaking on behalf of the Trade Justice Campaign before the December 2005 WTO meeting in Hong Kong, Nelson Mandela said: 'There is a chance to make decisions that will lift billions of people out of poverty. Trade can be part of the solution to poverty but at the moment it's part of the problem.'

The global campaign for trade justice continues in the wake of the failed Hong Kong talks where industrialized nations dragged their feet, refusing to lower subsidies and open the door to Southern exports. According to Filipino Congress member Walden Bello, the promise of a final phase-out date for Northern agricultural export subsidies was little more than window dressing. 'Even with the phase-out,' he writes, 'other forms of export support will allow the European Union to continue to subsidize exports to the tune of 55 billion euros after 2013.'[4]

Commenting on his own country's predicament, Bello notes: 'Three decades of export-oriented growth have resulted in trade accounting for some 30 per cent of gross domestic product. WTO-imposed liberalization has converted the country from a net food-exporting country into a net food-importing one... The main pillar of the economy is now the export of labor, with some 10 per cent of the country's 90 million people working and living outside the country.'[5]

Political leaders are feeling increased pressure to act on behalf of the world's poorest. Across Latin America, opposition to globalization has exploded since Brazil's 1998 economic crisis and the collapse of the Argentinean economy in 2002 – both of which were caused by hard-line IMF policies and meddling by financial speculators. Following the election of former labor activist Ignacio 'Lula' da Silva in Brazil, leaders opposed to market fundamentalism were elected in Argentina, Ecuador, Venezuela, Bolivia, Uruguay and Chile. (In early 2010 the more market-oriented Sebastian Pinera narrowly defeated Chile's Eduardo Frei.)

At the November 2005 Summit of the Americas in Buenos Aires, those nations spearheaded opposition to the proposed Free Trade Area of the Americas (FTAA), derailing plans to extend free trade from the Arctic to Patagonia. The dissenting nations rejected the US-led plan, claiming in the Summit's closing declaration that 'conditions do not exist to attain a hemispheric free-trade accord that is balanced and fair with access to markets and free of subsidies and distorted commercial practices.'

Those who control the global economy are taking note. As far back as 1999, at the Asia Pacific Economic Co-operation (APEC) meetings in New Zealand, then-US trade negotiator Charlene Barshefsky hinted that the single greatest threat to globalization is 'the absence of public support'. Her concerns are justified. There is now a worldwide citizens' movement to rethink the global economy from the ground up. It is a movement which is becoming stronger by the day. And it is premised on one shared, central truth. The only way to convince states to act in the interests of their people is to construct a system that will put humans back in control at the center of economic activity. This is an enormous project but one in which millions of people in scores of countries around the globe are actively engaged. What follows are a few of the ideas for change currently being debated.

Changing the system

Abolish the Bretton Woods institutions
The IMF, along with sister organizations the World Bank and the World Trade Organization, should be abolished – replaced with completely new organizations with new mandates and new staff.

The new agencies should be decentralized, regional institutions built on co-operative principles rather than free trade and capital mobility. They must become more democratic and more focused on the needs and interests of the citizens of the world rather than fixated on narrow market goals.

This regional approach is now being seriously considered.

The recent global financial crisis has prompted even mainstream political leaders to speculate about a new European equivalent of the IMF. When Greece's debt soared in early 2010, the country teetered on the brink of bankruptcy. The European Union's concern was the impact of the plunging Euro on the rest of the EU. The possible solution: a European equivalent of the IMF – a European Monetary Fund – to provide financial backing for Greece. 'We want to be able to resolve our problems in the future without the IMF,' said German Chancellor, Angela Merkel.

These new institutions will need to be more accountable to all their members – with more democratic and more transparent decision-making.

In the past the Fund has been arrogant and closed to criticism. New regionally based agencies would need to move beyond Finance Ministry officials to talk (and listen) to trade unions, peasant organizations, women's groups and non-governmental organizations

– the people who will be on the receiving end of the social impact of any agreement. To improve accountability, there should be regular external evaluations of whatever programs and policies are put in place.

Critically, structural adjustment policies – political, social and economic conditions attached to balance-of-payment loans – should be jettisoned. The drive for 'efficient markets' should not be allowed to erode national sovereignty or interfere with the decisions of elected governments. Coercion is not acceptable.

The central goal of these new regional organizations must be to improve the lives of ordinary people – to alleviate poverty, to wipe out Southern debt, to promote equity and to encourage efficient, green technologies. Markets should serve people, not the other way round.

As long as a global market economy exists – and it doesn't show any sign of disappearing soon – multilateral institutions will be necessary to regulate and manage the flow of capital, goods and services. But in the words of Keynes, we should 'minimize' rather than 'maximize economic entanglement among nations.'

Co-operation must be the watchword of any new regional institutions. A single-minded, inflexible approach based on market fundamentalism will exacerbate the instability and inequality of the global market. By scrapping the Bretton Woods trio – the IMF, the World Bank and the WTO – we can start afresh to build new institutions with a moral purpose and a democratic mandate which will work to the benefit of the majority of the world's citizens.

Support a tax on financial speculation

Unregulated investment has turned the global economy into a casino where speculators search for instant profits, ignoring the human consequences of their actions. Nowhere was this more evident than in the world-shaking financial crisis which began in late

2007. The combination of sub-prime mortgages, speculation and greed by banks, insurance companies and investment firms triggered the most severe economic downturn since the Great Depression. From September 2007 to March 2009, more than $50 trillion of assets were wiped out, including $7 trillion in US stock market wealth and $6 trillion in US housing wealth.[6]

Currency markets can be useful – taking the worry out of international buying and selling by figuring out today what a future purchase will cost. But it's estimated that just 2-4 per cent of currency trading has to do with real market exchanges. The rest is pure speculation, making money off money. A tax on speculative dealings in foreign currencies, shares and other securities would put people ahead of profits. In 1978, the Nobel Prize-winning economist James Tobin proposed that a small worldwide tariff (less than half of one per cent) be levied by all major countries on foreign-exchange transactions in order to 'throw some sand in the wheels' of speculative flows. The tax would have no effect on serious long-term investors. A tax of .05 per cent would dampen speculation while stabilizing global markets and capturing much-needed funds for global development. If the annual trade fell to $100 trillion after a transaction tax was imposed it would still yield revenues of $500 billion for the public purse.

There is a significant movement to back such a tax. Britain, France and Germany have all signaled support and in early 2010 more than 350 economists urged the G20 governments to adopt the so-called 'Robin Hood' tax as 'a matter of urgency'. The Columbia University economist, Jeffrey Sachs, says: 'The transaction tax is technically feasible and morally essential to repair the mess made by the banks.' The tax is designed to dampen speculation and to raise funds to support global development – a rare opportunity to capture the enormous wealth of an untaxed sector and redirect it towards the public good.

Redesigning the global economy

The main barrier to the global transaction tax is not technical, it's political. The tax is seen as a threat by the financial community and has met with stiff resistance by a sector with massive political clout. The very idea of putting people ahead of markets challenges the foundations of the current global economic model and those who control it.

Control capital for the public good

The world came a hair's breadth from complete economic collapse in 2007-09. Only a multi-billion dollar bailout by national governments helped stave off disaster. Globalization – the freewheeling era of unregulated capital flows and free markets – brought us to the brink. And we will bear the social and psychological scars for years to come. The costs of the crisis have been huge: industries have been shuttered, trade has plummeted, unemployment has spiked, hunger and deprivation have increased as the recession ripples around the globe.

In countries like Iceland and Ireland the bailouts of the banks cost more than two-and-a-half times the national income. As a result governments everywhere are faced with massive deficits which may haunt them for decades. Memories are short: already corporate executives and their political allies are planting the seeds of 'deficit fear', warning that we will all have to tighten our belts to pay for the malfeasance of the financial community. But we must not forget what caused the crisis in the first place: a globalized financial system which was unaccountable, unregulated, and driven by greed. Now is the time for a clean start. We have the greatest opportunity since the Depression of the 1930s to restructure global economic relations in a more democratic and sustainable way.

Here are some brief notes on alternative strategies for economic globalization that could begin now.

Regulate the financial system – Capital needs to be used as an instrument of development, not as a tool for turning a quick profit at the expense of people and the Earth. Democratic control of capital means strict regulation of banks and investment firms. Their purpose is to transfer money from savers to investors. They should not be in the business of gambling.

Close tax havens – They serve no useful purpose except to help corporations hide their profits and to make rich individuals even richer. They should be closed immediately and international rules should be put in place that allow tax officials in all countries to exchange financial information and to end banking secrecy.

Break up the big banks – If they're too big to fail they're too big, period. After the meltdown of 2008, governments in Britain, the US and elsewhere became part-owners of some of the biggest banks and insurance companies. But the crash also spawned even larger banks as winners swallowed losers. The big banks should be broken into smaller units so if they do fail they don't threaten the entire system. At the moment their gambling is risk-free; if they lose, taxpayers pick up the tab.

Fix foreign investment – Foreign investment should be welcome only if social obligations are met; governments should be able to restrict the repatriation of profits. Governments should also have the right to require corporations, both foreign and domestic, to meet basic social obligations and development priorities such as labor standards, job quotas, environmental safeguards and social-security contributions.

Promote public enterprise – Governments have a responsibility to use tax revenues for protecting the 'commons' through public investments. These could include: exercising public ownership over key sectors of the economy; establishing social programs and public services; safeguarding ecologically sensitive areas; and protecting cultural heritage.

Redesigning the global economy

People before profits – A foreign corporation could not demand compensation for an environmental law that placed a quota on the export of a nonrenewable resource or a health ban on the sale of toxic substances. Nor should a foreign company claim compensation for loss of future profits because government actions prevent a planned investment from going ahead.

Go local – The export-oriented model needs to be jettisoned and free trade reined in. The US can't continue as the consumer of last resort for global exports. Countries need to redirect production towards domestic needs. Trade policy, including tariffs and quotas, should be used to protect the local economy and to boost domestic manufacturing. This will both strengthen community bonds and benefit the environment.

Support fair trade

'Max Havelaar', the first fair trade initiative, was launched in Holland in 1988. The name was taken from a fictional character who had opposed the exploitation of coffee pickers in Dutch colonies. In 1997, the Fair Trade Labeling Organization (FLO) brought together Max Havelaar with counterparts in other countries. Today, the FLO operates in 19 countries in Europe, Japan, North America, Mexico, Australia and New Zealand/Aotearoa.

Compared with conventional trading structures, these Alternative Trade Organizations offer higher returns to producers in the developing world through direct trade and fair prices. The fair trade movement is a response to a global trading system that is both unjust and exploitative – global trading rules are rigged to benefit the rich and marginalize the poor. Fixing the global system will take major institutional changes and a determined campaign.

Unregulated trade allows corporations to pit workers against each another, to reduce the bargaining strength of trade unions, to strip away benefits, to ignore dangerous working conditions and to reduce wages.

Instead, trade agreements must bolster the rights of working people by promoting labor rights – including the freedom to form trade unions and bargain collectively. Free trade is a social issue as well as an economic one. To attract investors, countries compete to lower costs. That can trigger a 'race to the bottom' where job-hungry nations offer cheap labor, weak environmental laws, lax health and safety standards or reduced social services. Governments must have the right to regulate foreign investment to protect their citizens and to link investment to national development priorities.

Nations should have the power to establish and defend intellectual property rules that protect the interests of their citizens. Trade agreements must guarantee access to essential drugs, prohibit the erosion of traditional cultures and protect indigenous knowledge and biodiversity.

If democracy is to have meaning, citizens must help to formulate trade rules. These agreements must promote civil and political rights as well as the social, cultural, economic and environmental rights of peoples and communities.

In the meantime, the fair trade movement provides a chance to learn about the blatant unfairness of the global trading system. And to set standards that could redefine global trade to include social and environmental considerations.

1 *Asian Development Bank Outlook 2009*, Asian Development Bank, Manila 2009. 2 *State of the World 2006*, Worldwatch Institute, WW Norton, New York, 2006. 3 'Downside up', *New Internationalist*, No 430, Mar 2010. 4 Walden Bello, 'The Real Meaning of Hong Kong: Brazil and India Join the Big Boys' Club', www.focusweb.org, 22 Dec 2005. 5 Walden Bello, 'Reflections of a Filipino MP', *New Internationalist*, No 430, Mar 2010. 6 John Bellamy Foster, 'The Age of Monopoly-Finance Capital', *Monthly Review*, Vol 61, No 9. Feb 2010.

Contacts

International
ActionAid, www.actionaid.org
ATTAC (Association for the taxation of financial transactions for the aid of citizens), www.attac.org
Bretton Woods Project www.brettonwoodsproject.org
Focus on the Global South, www.focusweb.org
International Forum on Globalization, www.ifg.org
Third World Network, www.twnside.org.sg
Transnational Institute, www.tni.org
UN Development Programme, www.undp.org
World Social Forum, www.forumsocialmundial.org.br

Australia
Aftinet (Australian Fair Trade and Investment Network), www.aftinet.org.au

Canada
Canadian Centre for Policy Alternatives, www.policyalternatives.ca
Council of Canadians, www.canadians.org
Halifax Initiative, www.halifaxinitiative.org
Polaris Institute, www.polarisinstitute.org

New Zealand/Aotearoa
Oxfam New Zealand, www.oxfam.org.nz

United Kingdom
Jubilee Debt Campaign, www.jubileedebtcampaign.org.uk
New Economics Foundation, www.neweconomics.org
Oxfam, www.oxfam.org.uk
War on Want, www.waronwant.org
World Development Movement, www.wdm.org.uk

United States
Global Exchange, www.globalexchange.org
Institute for Food and Development Policy (Food First) www.foodfirst.org
Institute of Policy Studies, www.ips-dc.org
Public Citizen/Global Trade Watch, www.citizen.org/trade

Bibliography

Benjamin R Barber, *Jihad vs McWorld*, Ballantine Books, New York, 1995.

John Bellamy Foster and Fred Magdoff, *The Great Financial Crisis: causes and consequences*, Monthly Review Press, New York, 2009.

Walden Bello, *Dilemmas of domination: the unmaking of the American Empire*, Metropolitan Books, Henry Holt & Co, New York, 2005.

Herman E Daly and John B Cobb Jr, *For the Common Good*, Beacon Press, Boston, 1989.

Susan George, *Another world is possible if...*, Verso, London, 2004.

John Gray, *False Dawn: the delusions of global capitalism*, Granta Books, London, 1998.

David Korten, *The Post-Corporate World: life after capitalism*, Kumarian and Berrett-Koehler, San Francisco, CA and West Hartford, CT 1999.

John McMurtry, *The Cancer Stage of Capitalism*, Pluto Press, London, 1999.

George Soros, *The Crisis of Global Capitalism*, Perseus Books, 1998.

Peter Stalker, *The No-Nonsense Guide to Global Finance*, New Internationalist, Oxford, 2009.

Joseph Stiglitz, *Globalization and its discontents*, WW Norton, New York, 2003.

Joseph Stiglitz and Andrew Charlton, *Free trade for all: how trade can promote development*, Oxford University Press, Oxford/New York, 2006.

Joseph Stiglitz, *Freefall: America, free markets and the sinking of the world economy*, WW Norton, New York, 2010.

Eric Toussaint, *Your money or your life: the tyranny of global finance*, Haymarket Books, Chicago, 2006.

New Internationalist magazine, **www.newint.org**

Index

Index

CPSIA information can be obtained
at www.ICGtesting.com
Printed in the USA
LVOW10s0908250117
521976LV00011B/49/P